Live Happily on Less

52 Ideas to Renovate Your Life and Lifestyle

By Carolyn Henderson

Also by Carolyn Henderson

Grammar Despair: Quick, simple solutions to problems like, Do I say him and me or he and I?"

Life Is a Gift (Kindle)

The Jane Austen Driving School (Kindle)

(available at Amazon.com)

Dedication

To my tribe -- The Norwegian Artist, Eldest Supreme, Small One, College Girl, the Son and Heir, Tired of Being Youngest

We have learned, and continue to learn, about life, love, and spending money, together

Introduction

This is not an easy economy in which to live.

Regardless of what you do and where you do it, if you are an ordinary person who depends upon your wages for your support, you probably chafe each month at just how quickly those wages disappear: taxes, fees, insurance, utilities, clothing, food -- all of these elements rise at a rate that regularly outpaces what you are paid, and it is a constant struggle to keep up with it all.

Technically, there are two major ways to increase the amount of money available to your household:

1) Make more money

2) Spend less money

Most people consider Option 1 as the only option, and they add a part-time job here, a seasonal stint there, regular overtime at work, and operating a business on the side as a means of increasing the amount of resources for peanut butter that month.

But regardless of how hard you work, and how much energy and verve you've got, there still remain 24 hours in a day, and you really do need time for sleeping, eating, and bathroom breaks. Time with family, friends, and just yourself is nice as well.

So enter Option 2, and while I know you're trying as hard as you can already, and you just can't cut anymore, don't give up on the concept before we've even gotten started. Spending less is a lifestyle, and it is not something that you succeed with overnight.

One small change starts the process, and if the change works for you, it becomes permanent. Success breeds success, and once you've accomplished (or are in the process of accomplishing) one change, you start looking around for more. It becomes a game -- a challenge -- and you realize, "I'm not stuck with one unattractive way of solving my problems."

This book is a means to help you make these changes, and it consists of 52 chapters -- one for each week of the year -- discussing different ways of looking at and doing things. Not all of these ideas will be applicable to you, but maybe, as you read a chapter, a variation of the theme will start playing in your head, and you'll think, "I could do . . . this."

What this book is **not** is a series of weird, unsustainable, outlandish, stressful, nit-picky, and time-consuming money saving "tips," along the lines of extreme coupon clipping. Years ago, I read a book that advocated fixing the knees on blue jeans by undoing the inside and outside seams, tucking in a patch, then quickly sewing the whole thing back up again. It was fast and simple, the author assured me, and anybody truly interested in frugality would have no problem doing this.

Well, the pressure was on, so I tried it.

It was **not** fast, it was **not** simple, I never did it again, and I threw away the book that advocated it, because this was the easiest of the projects. (By the way, I know how to sew -- adequately.)

Just because someone says something is easy doesn't mean that it is. And there are a lot of people out there living extremely complicated lives in pursuit of their frugality. Me? I like living in the 21st century. My washing machine is my best friend, and I'm not going to be swishing clothes around in the bathtub anytime soon. I do, however, dry my clothes on a line -- always have -- and there's a rhythm to it that I've picked up over the years. You may recoil at this -- which is one reason why this book focuses less on definite, try-this-one-out techniques and more on a philosophical exploration of how to live, happily, on what you have.

Some of the techniques that work for me will be alien to you; some of the things that make sense to you will flummox me. The key thing about living well on less isn't so much a bullet point list of Do This and Don't Do That as it is changing the way you think -- about yourself, your lifestyle, and how you approach money. Only you can do this.

My job, in this book, is to walk with you for awhile, tell some stories on what has worked for us, and encourage you to think, think, think for yourself, outside the box, and unaffected by the glances, looks, attitudes, or behavior of your neighbors.

If you're like me, you'll sit down and read the whole book in one sitting while you're soaking in the bathtub, which is fine; I never could stop at just one Oreo cookie. Feel free to do so. Or just randomly open the book to a page and read. Or pick out what you like from the table of contents and peruse that.

Be aware that I am the married mother of four grown or nearly grown children, and much of my experience comes from living in a chaotic and noisy family. So, my slip may show now and then, and if you're single you may get frustrated with a couple of the chapters (Children Are Expensive comes to mind). But whether you live in a family of 10 or a family of 1, saving money and living well are issues of attitude, and each one of us is responsible for our own attitude, individually. It just gets more complicated the more people you have walking in and out of the front door each day.

The main thing is to start thinking differently about your life and lifestyle, understanding that there is no one "right" way to live, no one "perfect" job to strive for, no concept of failure because your car, or your house, or your dog, doesn't look like your neighbor's. That's called coveting, and whether you're a religious person or not, envying someone because of what they've got and you don't is always a bad idea.

You are you, and in this next year's process of making little changes in your life, you're going to get to know you very well. Enjoy doing so, and rejoice in what you are, recognizing that you are the only person who can fulfill being who you were meant to be.

4

If that sounds philosophical and not financial enough, bear with me. Living frugally, and well, is more than a matter of not spending money; indeed, many frugal people save up for some expensive, but worthwhile purchases -- fine art (I put that one first because I am co-owner of Steve Henderson Fine Art), Bactrian Camel hair yarn (I'm a knitter; get used to it -- it factors in a lot of stories), a very special wine, an exotic house plant, a grain grinder -- many times, these are items that your neighbor with the nicer car wouldn't dream of buying, but that's okay, because he's not you.

The Economics of Being Cool -- and Frugal

Being frugal is chic these days.

It's exhilarating to go to bed knowing that you're weird and out of step, and then burst into the kitchen the next morning as a dynamic, exciting, creative, green living, Chic woman of power and wisdom!

At no point in my life have I so easily transformed from one persona to another, and what's especially fun is that I haven't made a single, solitary change in my life. I wish that losing weight were this easy.

But it isn't, and neither is being frugal, actually, because despite all the articles urging us to Live Simply -- Go Green and the online 10 E-Z Bullet-Pointed Steps to Saving Money Now! living wisely and well is not something that we do overnight.

It's a lifestyle, a way of thinking which -- until the economy tanked and decided to stay down there wallowing in the mud -- was considered cheap and peculiar, not to mention a sign of failure because, as well all know, successful people own a lot of stuff.

But these days, successful people live within their income -- a pretty good trick as many people find their disposable income going down while their expenses keep going up.

And yet, they make little decisions that add up to a big impact: instead of takeout pizza, they slap ketchup, cheese, and a piece of pepperoni on an English muffin and toast their ingenuity with a glass of wine.

Or they stop for a micro-second, hand hovering over that DVD and ask themselves, "Do I really need this -- right now?" and they go home and think about it.

"You can talk yourself into anything; and you can talk yourself out of anything," my grandfather always said. He was a Realtor, and he saw this happen a lot.

"Often, the deciding factor in purchasing a house was relatively minor," he said.

Too often, before this new economy that none of us asked for and most of us wish would go away, or at least get over its flu, the deciding factor in a purchase was what other people would think.

But now, more and more people are liberating themselves from the tyranny of how they *think* other people think about them -- and they're considering what is uniquely best for them and their own families.

That's frugality -- that's where it starts -- reviewing the sensibility and wisdom of a purchase based upon one's own thoughts, desires, needs, and resources.

Years ago, we dropped a chunk of pennies on a wheat grinder which does exactly what it sounds like -- it grinds wheat berries into flour. People around us were buying phones.

Nowadays, their phones are broken, gone, out of date, while our wheat grinder keeps merrily grinding along, providing that someone is physically moving the wheel around and around. And we're cool.

"You grind your own wheat? That's really smart."

Smarter than your phone, actually.

We spent the same amount of money as our peers for an industrial quality clunk of metal that will never look cool, but it provides freshly ground flour for the freshly made bread that we produce in our kitchen. We eat really well.

Being frugal doesn't mean that you don't spend money. Many times, as with our wheat grinder, it involves making a major purchase.

But it means that you spend money wisely -- on something you want, will take pleasure in, and will use and enjoy for a long time to come. That could be a wheat grinder, a hank of Bactrian camel hair yarn, a work of art, or even a phone, if that's what you really, truly want -- the only thing for certain is that it won't necessarily look like what everyone else is getting.

Not if we're buying according to what we want and need, as opposed to what we think others expect us to have.

This week, think about yourself, and the things you like to do, and the things you don't like to do. Do you ever buy things because you feel as if you were expected to do so? And do you not buy something you really want, because you're afraid of what other people will say?

Just being aware is the first step, and we become aware by asking ourselves questions -- something easy to avoid in today's society because we allow ourselves so little time, or silence, in which to think. This is where washing dishes by hand, or weeding, or dusting come in handy -- boring, mindless jobs that get something done without engaging too much of our thought process.

Survival Mode

When you think about saving money, it's important to ask yourself why. If you've lost your job, no income is coming in, and you're living off of your savings until you can pick up work, then you're in survival mode. This is different from still working, getting a paycheck, and wanting to cut back so that you can put more in savings or just not spend your entire income.

People frequently confuse the two concepts, and unless they're questioning every purchase, eating oatmeal twice a day (and dry toast for dinner), and darning their acrylic 12-pairs-in-a-pack socks, then they feel as if they are failing somehow.

But this type of extreme saving -- like 1200 calorie diets -- is difficult to maintain in the long term. While it's a necessary component when you're in survival mode, it's an emotional and time sapping burden when you're still working and meeting the bills. And you get tired of it.

If you are, however, in survival mode, you will find yourself getting remarkably creative about how you spend -- or don't spend -- your money, simply because you don't have enough of it. Impulse buying is naturally curbed by the constant thought in the back of your mind, "I need enough to pay the electric bill. I don't really need a vanilla scented candle, even if it is 75 percent off."

You do this over, and over, and over, in every store -- questioning every single expenditure for its necessity, minimizing purchases, walking away from Buy One Get

10

One Half Off shoe purchases because, as much as you'd like a new pair of sandals, the flip flops you have on still work, and you don't really NEED new shoes. If you were not in survival mode, you'd reconsider, because your flip flops aren't going to last forever, and it would be prudent to have a pair of footwear in reserve, but when you're in survival mode, you're betting that the flip flops will make it. And if they don't, you'll glue them/tie them/staple them back together.

When you're in survival mode, you scour yard sales, second hand stores, and the homes of your family and friends for low priced or free merchandise that can keep you from having to buy anything. While being in survival mode isn't especially pleasant, it does alter your perception on issues, and you realize that you really don't need as much stuff as you previously thought you did. If you carry this thought forward into the day when you're out of survival mode -- and although this feels as if it will never come, circumstances do eventually improve -- you find it easier to get by with less.

However, if you are not in survival mode and you approach every purchase -- or non-purchase -- as if you were, you can be really irritating to live around. Cheap, penurious, parsimonious -- survival-mode savers who don't need to be question pennies, which is why we call them penny pinchers. Ironically, they worry so much about saving small amounts in small areas, that they wind up spending more -- think about the person who drives 10 miles to another store to save 5 cents a pound on bananas.

11

You also have to ask yourself why you're putting yourself through this: down on this earth, you get one shot through, and if your situation is such that you enjoy, reasonably, what you do, and you get a sufficient amount from it to pay for a roof over your head, eat, and, keep a medium-sized dog just because you want to, then why live as if you were going to be kicked out onto the sidewalks tomorrow?

If you read books or blogs on frugality, you've no doubt encountered this attitude of extreme saving, accompanied by a touch of self-righteousness that gently but firmly condemns anyone who doesn't think, or spend, the way the writer does. I do not like these books or blogs -- the tone of them is joyless, dour, reproachful, critical, harsh, and stern -- and while the authors may be saving money, they're sure not enjoying the fruits of their labor. They are, however, eccentric -- not the fun, my Aunt Edith is sweetly different type of eccentric, but the, "Wow. I do not want to be alone in the same room with this person" type of eccentric.

- It's okay to have a bottle of nice wine -- sure, water's free, but it's not the same. (Our family is remarkably adept at enjoying cheap wine, and we tell ourselves that, if we get used to the expensive stuff, then we'll know what we're missing. But since we don't know what we're missing, we enjoy our cheap wine.)

- It's okay to buy fresh flowers for your table -- yes, you can go out in the fields and find them for free, but if you don't have any fields handy, then this isn't an option for you. It's also difficult in January, in Minnesota. As with food, buy flowers with the

12

season, and if carnations are $3.99 a bunch and roses $15.99, then go for the carnations (they last longer). Or buy a small plant for $3.99 and enjoy it while it's blooming; afterwards you can plant it in your yard or give it to someone who will.

- It's okay to go out to lunch for a sub sandwich instead of bringing celery sticks from home.

- It's okay to buy a new pair of jeans, and wear the torn-knees version in the garden. You don't have to spend two hours patching them up. Or turning them into a purse.

- It's okay to enjoy an outlandishly priced coffee concoction drink, complete with sprinkles, and you can do it out in the open where people will see you.

Obviously, if you're in true survival mode, you forego a lot of these luxuries, because when you're truly worried about meeting the mortgage, wine is a luxury. (That being said, even in survival mode you break down and treat yourself, but you do it much more cheaply than you do when the mortgage is secure. Remember that cheap wine I mentioned up above? It is possible to get a decent bottle in the $2.99 range. Really. As long as you're not picky.)

But when you're not in survival mode, and you're just trying to control the flow of money out of your household, then the fun little luxuries of life are fine. The important thing is to recognize those little luxuries for what they are -- luxuries -- and when we enjoy luxuries on a regular basis, they are no longer special in our mind. We begin to think of them as necessities.

Which means that the wine, the flowers, the lunch out, the coffee -- these are special things that, purchased too frequently, add up to become a drain on our finances. But on occasion, and celebrated as the extras that they are, the treats and extras that we buy ourselves and the people we love are things to celebrate, a joyous addition to life itself.

This week, review the luxuries of your life. Don't be a fanatic about it, but throughout the day, observe where your money is going, and ask yourself just how often your money goes in that direction. If you have a vaguely uncomfortable feeling that money just disappears too quickly, then listen to this -- maybe you are buying too many treats and thinking of them as necessities.

If this is so, then consider making adjustments -- slowly, not cutting yourself off from everything at once, because this is the best way to ensure that you'll give up on the whole project before the week is out.

And if you've been reading tips on frugality that make you feel as if you are a failure because you've never stapled all of your office waste paper into a cheap, free drawing tablet for your children, then put the book away. This author's problems, and hang-ups, do not have to become your own.

Learn to listen to yourself, and recognize that deep gut feeling of discomfort. If you find yourself thinking, "I can't do this -- it's too much!" then step back, pull away, and

14

give yourself time to think and process what you're reading and seeing.

Many times that deep gut feeling of discomfort is dead on accurate, telling us that something isn't right. Too frequently, however, we push forward, ignoring that feeling because, we tell ourselves, "It's just feelings."

Replace the word "feelings" with "instinct," and you'll have a more accurate assessment. Listen to your instincts.

Getting Along Nicely with Others

In the introduction I mentioned that my background is the mother of four children, and much of what I've learned has been within a noisy, chaotic household. Even the nicest children (like ours) are always demanding something, and depending upon their age and circumstance, you are faced with continuous requests for purchases that simply must be made.

If you're married, you have a spouse, which I'm sure you've noticed, and that spouse may think differently about money than you do. If you've ever taken any financial class or seminar, you may have found yourself and your spouse labeled -- You are a mighty Lion, commanding and taking control of the family finances, careful about the charge card use and insistent that your spouse not make major purchases without discussing it with you first.

Your spouse is a Terrier dog, running playfully through the stores and online catalogs, picking up anything that attracts the eye and dragging it home, dropping it on the front porch with a happy sigh.

The major aspect I detest about labeling is that the people who set up the labels generally put themselves in the best group -- like the Lion, which, when you think about it, may be King of the Beasts, but is not the most giving, sensitive creature around. The labelers never bring this aspect up, though, I've noticed.

(As an aside, years ago one of our daughters participated in an activity in which everyone was put into one of four groups. The leader, of course, was a lion -- and interestingly, was an extremely insensitive, thoughtless man, although he had no idea this was so. Our daughter wound up being a Labrador Retriever -- seriously, a DOG? -- which did little for her self-esteem. Eschew labels. You are more than a lion or a dog; or Winnie the Pooh or Eeyore; or Aragorn or Frodo. You are a multifaceted being with various skills and abilities, and the way you look at finances is more complex than what you can stuff into a stereotype.)

Without labeling yourself or anyone else in your household, it's important to realize that we all think differently, something that anyone who has tried to order pizza for a group of six people quickly figures out. You may be more cautious in your spending habits than your spouse/partner/friend/significant other, which may be why you're the one reading this book. Or the two of you may think fairly similarly, which is great if you both think carefully about your finances, not so great if you're both whimsical and spontaneous and devil-may-care.

The point is, if there is more than one of you in the household -- spouse, child, friend, just some other human being -- then you don't make decisions in isolation, and you are not an island floating through the sea of finances commanding each and every decision. You have to talk about how you spend money, and on what, and even if you are the major person controlling the funds -- as in you're the grown up and the only other person in the household is an eight-year-old child -- you will still be influenced and pressured by this other person's demands and needs.

Communicate with one another. As you learn new ways of thinking, or as you identify how you think already, discuss

17

this with the other members of your household. Obviously, you won't go into as great of detail with a three-year-old as you will with another adult of equal status, but if you want to try different things, at least let others know what you're thinking, and why. Teenagers are especially sensitive to wanting to look like others (I know, this is a stereotype, but it runs pretty true), and if your financial decisions jeopardize purchases that they consider crucial, they are old enough to dialogue with you about their opinions and yours. If you keep your mind as open as you want theirs to be, they can provide insight and suggestions from a completely different perspective.

I mean this, by the way. Our Son and Heir, at 18, became absolutely committed to the idea that we needed another goat; our two existing ones were . . . older, and not producing milk at the level that he thought we needed. So he brought up the idea every meal, before or after he mentioned that we needed ducks and a half-dozen turkeys. He had all sorts of arguments to prove his point, but ultimately, his actions were the deciding factor.

He tracked down a seller of goats, rode his bicycle out 10 miles to their farm, reviewed the animal (as the principle person who did the milking, he knew what he was looking for) negotiated a price, and bought the thing himself -- after checking with us that we wouldn't mind the gift. The 1-2 gallons of milk we then started receiving each day he parceled out as pet food to the cats and dogs, and he learned to make cheese.

Then he moved to Alaska for five months and left us with the goat and all that milk, but that's another story.

The point is, he had a number of good points, and an equal number of counterpoints to any of our many arguments. Eventually, he carried the day because he answered all of our objections. He thought the purchase over from its initial financial outlay and the extra amount that a new animal would cost in hay, feed, and housing; and he showed how the benefits outweighed the expenses -- the majority of which, in the purchase of the goat -- he was willing to front.

(If you have kids, don't hide your finances from them. From a young age, discuss what you spend and how, and teach them, on a daily basis, what spending and saving money looks like. Each of my four children has memories of my sitting at the dining room table, filling out checks for the monthly bills, and as time went by I answered their questions about checking accounts, debit cards, charge accounts, monthly expenses -- so that as they grew into teenagers, they had an awareness of the possibilities and limitations of money. This crucial life skill isn't something you want to leave in the hands of your local high school's Life's Living Skills class.)

Figure out what your spending/saving philosophy is, and question the other members of the household to figure out theirs, especially if they write checks off of the same account. The more that household members communicate with one another, the more that 1) you will learn from one another and 2) you will work together toward common goals, in this case, spending the household income wisely.

Pots and Pots of Money

I chatted with a young woman the other day who told me about an online teaching position she had just secured, and her major commentary on the matter was this:

"I'll make pots and pots of money at this place, and I really don't have to do much of anything."

Wow. Everybody's dream job.

Let me clarify myself:

While it's a laudable intent to maximize the amount of money you make per hour -- that's sensible, and most of us in ordinary jobs probably feel that we're not paid what we're really worth (and we're probably not) -- this woman's cynicism is a soul killer.

In discussing the new position, it became very clear that she had little respect for her clients, and her major goal was to run through as many of them as she could, as quickly as she could, so that she could do what she really wanted to do -- post on Facebook, maybe?

At no time did she express any satisfaction or pride in what she was doing, and her major comment to me, when I remarked that I could not get a position like this -- even though learning-wise I was as qualified as she -- because I didn't have the necessary degree was,

"You didn't go through the system. In order to succeed, you've got to go through the system."

Sadly, in this economy of ours, in which we create less and less, and the jobs that pay money are linked to administrative, managerial, and degree-laden positions, if you opt to not follow the rules and leap the hurdles, you do find yourself on the outside, looking in at people drawing large salaries for jobs that we can't necessarily identify.

And those people, like this woman, will call you stupid -- based pretty much on your lack of significant income and refusal to play the game.

If you are one of these people who didn't play the system, be encouraged -- you are not stupid. Your worth and intelligence and value are not based upon your annual salary or monthly wage. While you often wish that either of those could be more (so do people like this woman, incidentally; no matter how much they make, it never seems to be enough), you can live as fruitful of an existence as my Woman of the System, and maybe more -- not materially, necessarily, but a fruitful life consists of more than material possessions.

Start this week by determining that you will not define who and what you are by your job. When you are tempted to say, "I'm a bit of a failure, in so far as being a financial provider," please stop. If you work each day -- and this includes homemakers who don't generate an income at all, or persons stringing together a series of part time jobs to make ends meet, or someone who has a degree in one thing but is working in another field -- then you are not a failure. You are a valuable person doing good things. That you

21

don't make pots and pots of money at them has less to do with you than it does with The System.

And if you're tempted to think that you're dumb because you didn't play the System, don't. Eventually, The System chews people up and spits them out -- many of them in their 50s, being downsized from a dehumanizing office cubicle position from which they longed to escape but wished it had been more on their terms.

Any honest work is honorable. Our grandparents knew this, because during the Great Depression it was more important to keep food on the table and a roof over their heads than it was to impress others by material ostentation. As we became more and more affluent, we forgot this, and our goals adjusted gradually to include more purchases of more stuff, simply because we could.

Well, our national affluence goes up and down, and for many in this country these days, it's down. There is no shame in not being rich, and you're definitely not alone in this state of being.

Take a few minutes by yourself throughout the week and think about who you are -- outside of what you do to secure wages each day. Explore your personality, get in touch with the things that make you laugh and cry, look at the household and family members with whom you interact daily and tell yourself, "These are my tribe. We interconnect together."

These elements define you more strongly than any letters after your name, direct-deposited paycheck into your account, or curriculum vita.

Why does this matter? Because as you make changes in your life to start saving money, you're going to look different from the people around you. And as long as you're concerned about how you look different from the people around you, the changes that will be beneficial for you to make will be too difficult for you to stick to.

Get used to being different. It's a major component of living well.

The Big Stuff

Your house. Your car. Insurance payments -- life, health, auto, home. College loans.

Some expenses are fixed, and generally they're the big ones. Unfortunately, when we look to save money, it comes out of the areas that mean the most to us and make a genuine impact on the quality of our lives -- what we eat, what we wear, how we entertain ourselves.

Whether or not you feel the benefit of your property, sales, or income taxes -- they won't go away, and if you want to decrease them, investing into some time with an accountant may pay off. We ourselves take our yearly taxes to an accountant, and the amount he saves more than makes up for the amount he charges.

(By the way, as a controversial aside, if you feel that you are paying too much in taxes, then consider voting "No" on the various bonds floating around, one of the few opportunities when the citizens being taxed have a small say about the matter. Yes, schools and fire departments and police stations and road repair are all important, but tax-dependent entities also do not -- or should not -- have carte blanche. As long as we keep voting yes, for everything, all the time, our taxes will remain high, and our "services" will not necessarily reflect what we think we're paying for.)

Your car -- or cars. Do you need all of them? It's a question worth asking. At one time, we had three vehicles -- all paid for -- so it's difficult justifying getting rid of them, but they all required insurance, upkeep, yearly tabs and gasoline, and we questioned whether we really needed to keep sinking money into these areas. Eventually, we worked ourselves down to one vehicle.

Maybe you need multiple cars -- but maybe you don't. At least review the concept.

Your house -- this is the single largest purchase that most of us make, and if you're paying a mortgage, you're not just paying a mortgage. Hidden in those monthly payments are your property taxes (which is why most people don't realize just how much they're paying in this area) and possibly mortgage insurance. Regarding the latter, which many lending institutions impose on the buyer if you make your home purchase with less than 20 percent deposit, you can request your lender to stop the private mortgage insurance payments once your equity -- the amount of the home that you actually own, and do not owe on -- is greater than 20 percent.

In other words, if your home is worth $300,000, once you have paid off $60,000, then approach your lender about canceling the mortgage insurance, which, incidentally, is something that benefits the lender, not you. If you default on your loan, then the insurance kicks in -- for the lender.

If you have not already received an amortization schedule of your payments from your lender, ask for one. This schedule, which can be reflected upon monthly payment coupons that you use to make your mortgage payments, shows you how much your payment is, and how much of the amount for a particular month goes to pay interest and, most importantly, principal -- which is what you want to pay off as quickly as possible.

And herein, my friend, is where you can make a small but definite impact in the paying off of this very large, very long-term loan:

Make extra payments.

Any amount each month that is above your total mortgage payment -- and which you designate toward the principal -- cuts down the amount of interest you owe.

Look at this way, let's say your monthly payment is $1500, and this month, $200 of that goes to pay off the principal, and $1300 goes toward interest. If you make a $25 extra payment, then next month, you won't owe interest on that particular $25. Make another $25 extra payment the next month, and there's another $25, added to the first $25, that you don't owe interest on.

Over the course of a year, your $300 in extra payments represent $300 extra dollars toward the principal, and which you don't owe interest on.

Does that not sound like much? Maybe not -- so make a bigger payment. At one time, on a land payment of $300, I added $200 -- and something that was supposed to take 20 years to pay off took considerably less than that. We OWN our house and land (barring those irritating property taxes), and we accomplished this by making extra payments.

So if $25 is too little and $200 is too much, pick a number that works for you -- but whatever it is, make it -- because every dollar that you put toward principal is a dollar that isn't paying interest. When we made our payments, interest varied between 8 and 11 percent, so not paying interest on an amount, any amount, added up quickly. But even when rates are low, interest adds up, and especially in the first years of the loan, tipping the principal balance in your favor is a good thing.

This week? If you've got a mortgage, make an extra payment of . . . anything. Just get it started -- it's fun, month by month, watching the numbers change, and if you compare your original payment schedule with what happens when you make those extra payments, you find yourself wanting to write a bigger check the next month.

Listen to the Experts -- with a Grain of Salt

Back in the days when we had mortgages and made extra house payments, a very intelligent and very sincere financial adviser chided me about those payments.

"You should be buying stock or mutual funds," he told me. "They're getting a lifetime rate of 19 percent, which is considerably more than you're paying out in mortgage interest."

You will, like me, observe that the financial adviser received a commission on any stock or mutual funds purchases I made, whereas he received nothing on the extra payments I made on the house.

Understood.

He was also a person of genuine integrity, so I recognized that he sincerely believed in what he was telling me.

But I don't like to be in debt, because life changes, and the job you're depending on today is downsized tomorrow, and I didn't want to owe money on our principal place of residence -- and risk losing it all back to the bank -- if I didn't have to. I wanted the house paid off.

So I continued making those extra payments, and I did not invest in stocks and mutual funds.

And eventually, one day, everything was paid off. And shortly after that, the Norwegian Artist -- our principal breadwinner -- was downsized from his job.

No job. No secure monthly income. No direct-deposited, regular check.

But, also, no mortgage payments. So while we had to worry about what we were going to eat and how we were going to pay for electricity and -- man, this one irritates me -- how we were going to make our twice yearly contribution to the king for the privilege of living in the house and on the property we worked so hard to own -- we didn't have to worry about a foreclosure statement.

Our financial adviser -- our intelligent, sincere financial adviser -- was wrong.

What this goes to show is that, while you may not be an expert in an area, you're not dumb, and you know things about your finances, your family, your comfort zone, your situation that others do not, and you take those elements into consideration when you make a decision.

Trust yourself a little more. That's your task this week.

Let's finish out this chapter with *What Does It Take to Be an Expert?*, an article I published on my This Woman Writes site:

What Does It Take to Be an Expert?

I have no letters after my name.

Okay, officially I have a B.A., which in today's climate stands less for Bachelor of Arts as it does for Buy Additional -- credits, tuition, college time -- leading to more letters (like M.A. or PhD) if you actually want to get a job in the field. I think the B.A. might qualify me to work at a fast food restaurant, but since the degree was in English and not mathematics, I'm not officially educated to run the cash register.

In a society that equates letters after one's name with expertise in the subject, I am constantly reminded of my lack of credentials and subsequent inability to express my opinion on anything other than the train dream sequence in Theodore Dreiser's *Sister Carrie*, and whether or not this represents the loss of the heroine's virginity. (Do you care? I don't.)

If only I had taken a different path and spent a little longer listening to bored, ready-to-retire-tenured-professors reading from 10-year-old notes, I could have earned enough letters after my name to officially enable me to say something about raising kids.

For awhile, I wrote for one of those ShallowInformationPresentedInListForm.Com sites -- you know, the ones that pay 2 cents or so for every thousand hits -- and an especially enthusiastic editor continued to send back an article I had written about communicating with teenagers. Having lived through two and currently working through two more, I figured I had some experience in this area.

She didn't see it this way, critiquing me for making generalized statements like,

"They don't need you to be their buddy. But neither do they want you to be the authoritarian figure you were when they were two."

According to the editor, I was unqualified to make this statement. However, "If an expert says it, that is different."

Oh.

Years ago, when Eldest Supreme was a newborn trying to figure out breastfeeding from a woman whose only experience with milk was that it came in plastic jugs or waxed cartons, I turned to the experts. This is what I found:

1) A 60-year-old male pediatrician who recommended that I "stick the baby in her bassinet in the backroom, shut the door, and get on with your life. She's not nursing? Give her a bottle. You're just no good at producing milk."

2) A 22-year-old unmarried, childless, sibling-free health department social worker with a master's in early childhood nutrition. "It looks like you just can't produce proper breast milk. Half of today's women have this issue. You'll have to use formula."

Fortunately, a friend of mine introduced me to an actual expert, a woman with eight children who had breast fed each and every one of them. Because she was just a mom who stayed home and didn't really do anything and had no proper education in anything regarding children other than actually raising them, she had no letters after her name.

She did have good advice, though.

Within 24-hours I had a happy, full-of-breast-milk (mine!) baby that contentedly suckled (isn't that a quaint word?) for two-and-a-half years. Three more breast-milk-sated babies followed.

Sometimes, the experts are valuable. The auto mechanic comes to mind, and I do like my ophthalmologist. But other times it helps to remember that letters after a name are just that -- letters -- and they are not necessarily accompanied by a true interest in the field, a voracious desire to read and keep up with research, or, most significantly, common sense.

That latter is one we can all cultivate, regardless of our educational path. It seems to be missing these days.

Cutting up Your Charge Cards -- Do You Need to Do This?

Years ago, 95 percent of the adults in a church we were then attending participated in a video-conference financial workbook study program in which the guru advocated cutting up the charge cards and paying for everything with cash.

We were in the five percent that chose to not pay a fee to further enrich the guru; the rest of the five percent were in a vegetative state or were near dying, so financial secrets known only to the guru were of no interest to them. (Interestingly, I'm betting that the guru himself used some form of credit arrangement for his own life -- surely he didn't send his secretary with a bundle of cash to pay for his plane tickets, his hotel rooms, his dinners out, his rental car? -- but this wasn't the kind of statement one made to the 95 percent.)

So, is the guru right? Should you cut up your charge cards?

We haven't. But we also don't carry a balance. We pay off every month's charge as it comes, and we don't charge anything unless we have the money in the bank -- right then -- to pay it off.

This way, we enjoy all of the benefits conferred by a charge account -- the ability to pay for things over the Internet,

Thank You points, cash credit back, a good credit score, additional warranty protection for purchases -- without paying for it through interest incurred. We also don't use any cards that charge us a yearly fee.

For awhile, charge card companies offered free cards that carried an initial balance at 0 percent interest -- indefinitely -- as long as you made a minimum number of new charges each month. At the time, we owed $5,000 on our land, and I was tired of paying 7 percent interest, so I transferred the land balance to one of these cards and made my 3 minimum charges each month.

It was a game, a bet almost -- the charge company figured that I would miss making one of those charges, and if so, they could impose 20 percent interest on the unpaid balance. I was betting that I would remember, and that I could pay the amount off at $100 per month, freeing our resources for other purchases.

I won.

For four years I made three new charges -- small ones, because interest accrued on new charges -- and my monthly purchase of a banana, a cup of yogurt, a pack of gum covered something I was going to get anyway, and kept my 0 percent agreement intact. I scheduled my purchases around bill paying time, and if I appeared to forget, one of the kids -- some as young as 7 -- would remind me. They probably wanted the pack of gum.

So, if everybody did this, the charge card companies would fail, right?

Well, in the first place, not everybody will do this. If the offers exist and the benefits are there, the only person you have to worry about taking advantage of them is you.

Because, you see, the charge card companies aren't going to fail. They're businesses, big business, and everything they do is to ensure that they make more and better and bigger business. If they choose to offer 3 percent back on all of your gasoline purchases, they're not losing money, because they're betting that the average person will carry a revolving balance on their cards, and the charge companies will more than make up for in interest what they pay out in gas credits.

If you are one of those people with a revolving account, and if you charge for items without having the money to pay for it at the end of the month, then yes, you might want to think about cutting up your cards and not using them anymore. You don't need a financial guru to tell you that.

If you owe money on these cards, pay it off, because, while mortgage rates can get down pretty low, the charge cards don't look like they're going to lower their interest rates anytime soon. In the same way you make an extra payment on your house, make extra payments on those cards, and get that balance down and out of your life. Don't charge anything new unless you can pay for it.

Then, once you're down to zero, consider whether you have the type of personality that can use the cards for your benefit, and not that of the company that issues them. If the answer's no, then get out the scissors. If the answer's maybe, then make a plan -- how will you make charges and ensure that you can pay for them the month they're due? It doesn't matter if you get 2 percent cash back on clothing purchases online -- if it takes you 10 months to make the payments, you will have eaten up any money you made by the interest you've paid.

Get out of debt. You probably won't be able to accomplish that within this week, but at the very least, make the commitment.

Think of charge cards as what they are -- a short term, high interest loan, that enables you to purchase items without having to carry a lot of cash around. As long as you pay the balance off every month, you enjoy the convenience of the card and any other perks that come with it, like Thank You Points. Over the years, I have purchased numerous small appliances -- the vacuum cleaner, a microwave, part of my washing machine, the steam mop -- through the redemption of Thank You Points, and because I pay off my balance every month and never pay interest, I come out ahead on the deal.

Use the card for your advantage -- not that of the companies that issue them. This is one area where being different pays off in obvious, tangible ways.

Get out of Debt

There are so many ways to owe money in this society, and we're so used to them, it seems normal.

I remember one conversation with a woman who lived in a new housing development, with two new cars, one of which was an SUV to transport around her one child and a couple bags of groceries. She was young (30s -- that seems young to me), college educated, well dressed, and sitting in a living room of exquisitely matched furniture and tastefully accessorized decor -- I felt as if I were in Pier One Imports.

"I don't know anybody with a personal debt of less than $25,000," she told me. "I mean, that's in addition to house payments, car payments, college loan payments, oh, whatever else payments there are. I mean, that's just normal life these days."

No, it isn't.

It doesn't have to be.

In the next sentence she confessed to lying awake at nights, wondering what would happen to them if she or her husband lost their jobs, because they needed both jobs just to **not** keep up on all the purchases that they were making.

"But I guess that's normal, too," she sighed.

No, it isn't.

And then she went on to say that they were considering buying a boat, so that they could save money on vacations by going to cheaper places, with lakes, and having fun that way.

Seriously, this woman was real, and she has literally bought -- on credit -- into our media-saturated society's illusion that we can all live the way that people do on the movies -- "ordinary people," none of whom work at Wal-Mart but all seem to have high-paying managerial positions at unidentifiable businesses, and whose eight-room apartments are bigger than the average family's house.

You can't have it all. You cannot live materialistically on $20,000 as if you made $100,000, but that doesn't stop us all from trying, or feeling bad about ourselves when we "fail."

Whatever you make, live on it -- better yet, try to live on less. Tuck aside a $10 bill every month for emergencies; if you make more, tuck away more. But if you are constantly spending more than you make, switching from one charge card to another, not answering phones because it might be a collection agency, stop the madness now, and focus on pulling yourself out of debt.

Don't go into this feeling like a victim -- someone who's such a loser that you don't make enough, or that you work the wrong kind of job and can't get the income you deserve, or that you just can't get a handle on your finances.

Look at your fixed expenses first -- housing, transportation, insurance, taxes, utilities -- and see if you can bring any of them down. Can you refinance your home? Drive less? Get rid of the comprehensive and collision on your auto insurance (if your car is more than 10 years old, you probably don't need it)? Turn on fewer lights? Wash your clothes in cold water as opposed to warm or hot?

Some of the things you do save big chunks, others little, but they all add up.

And then, after you've looked at the fixed expenses, look at the flexible ones -- entertainment tops the list, and it's usually the first one to take the cuts. Food -- yes, we have to eat, but how or where makes a difference. Clothing, decor, electronics -- all of these are flexible. We'll be looking at these areas throughout the book, and while some of my suggestions will work for you, others won't -- but the key is not so much to give you MY way of doing things, as to encourage you to find YOURS.

Where you save and when you save, put money toward getting out of debt, because once you're not making interest payments any more, you've technically increased your take home pay.

Give yourself time to do this, by the way. It took time to get into debt, and it will take time to get out of it. As tempting as it is to announce that every single penny that isn't 100 percent necessary is going to pay off the debt, you won't be able to keep up this form of austerity for very long -- years and years, say. At some point you will feel deprived and resentful, taking it out on yourself and your budget by making some wildly inappropriate purchase.

Set up a realistic amount to reduce your debt; don't incur any additional debt; and keep steadily chipping your way through the rocks.

Buy This -- Now

I've never used a debit card. I watch people use them and pocket their receipt, and I think -- "Do you keep track of what you spend? Do you know how much you've spent in movie rentals this month?"

Maybe they do. Maybe they bank online and run through their purchases and put it all into an Excel file and review it at the end of the month.

But they probably don't.

I make most of my purchases with duplicate checks, which means that there is a carbon reference of every check written, and a couple times a month I sit down with an old fashioned ledger and enter in what I've purchased and where. On the left side of the book, I identify whether the purchase was for food, insurance, utilities, car, housing, clothing, savings, and, because we live on acreage, animal feed.

After years of doing this, I've internalized when I spend too much in one area or another, and if I need to purchase extra clothes for some child one month, I keep this in mind when I buy groceries (skip the wine this week; Nutella can wait until next month); gas (forget about the extra trip to the Big Town); or online purchases (the every-two-months tea order can wait another two weeks; we'll make more batches with the same leaves and drink a weaker brew).

The important thing is this: I know how much we have available to spend each month, and I know how much we generally spend, where. I also know, at any random time, how much we have in the checking account. If it's toward the end of the month and we've been doing pretty well, then I'm comfortable with a small impulse buy; but if it's the beginning of the month and the auto insurance premium went up from last time and the electric bill was higher than normal, then I pull back.

Know your income. Know how you spend it. Keep within it.

If you don't know where your money goes each month, start this week by finding out. Any office store will have an old-fashioned ledger; generally the pages on one side of the book are for writing out what you spent, where, and figuring out the balance in your account. The other side of the page has columns for identifying categories for that expenditure -- housing, food, utilities, car, insurance, taxes, gifts, savings, clothing, miscellaneous -- you choose the categories that work for you, and because there are a limited number of spaces on the ledger -- no more than eight -- you don't have to micro-identify every penny. Too many resources that tell you to set up a budget make the process so onerous and exhausting that you're done before you've started. If this is the case, the budget isn't doing you much good, is it?

The purpose of the budget, and the budget book, is to track where you're spending your money, and if you're off a few dollars here and there, don't panic. Just record what you spend -- by check, debit card, cash, or credit -- and if you can manage to do this for one month, you'll know more than you did before you started.

If you relax and avoid making the process too convoluted -- as people do when they panic about completing a series of workbook pages -- then you may stick with it over several months, and thereby get a stronger idea of how you spend your money over the year.

Buy one of these ledgers, now.

If you recoil at the thought of writing things down on paper with a pen, then set up an Excel file. If that's still too old fashioned, then find a reasonably priced budgeting software program that works for you and use it. Even if you do your banking online, take time to identify the eight or so major areas where your money goes.

If you don't know where it's going, then you can't figure out how to keep more of it closer to you.

You Do Not Save Money by Spending Money

At one of my favorite grocery stores, each transaction ends by the clerk handing me the receipt with a flourish and the statement, "You saved $56.35 by shopping with us today."

The idea is that the sales are so incredibly good, that if I had shopped anyplace else, I would have spent $56.35 more. Some days, I actually save more than I spent, sort of.

No matter how much money you save, however, you are still spending money, and if you buy something you don't really need or never really use, then you haven't saved any money at all.

Years ago, when we were wretchedly poor college students, The Norwegian Artist and I used to get together with another couple and shop for clothes at a discount outlet. To be more accurate, my girlfriend and I spent hours trying things on in the dressing rooms while our husbands kept rolling their eyes at one another and wondering how much longer this would last.

Each potential purchase was more deliciously tempting than the last, because each price tag had the original price -- $35 -- crossed out in red and replaced by the deep discounted sale price -- $8.95, a savings of nearly $26! At this rate, we could buy four items for the price of one, resulting in a phenomenal savings of money!

We bought bags and bags of clothes that didn't particularly fit because they were such an incredible bargain, and because they didn't particularly fit (mainly because they were cheaply made and shoddily put together), we rarely wore what we purchased. Although the price tag said that the items were worth $35, it's questionable whether they were worth the revised price of $8.95, and considering that they moved from the sales bag to our closet to the second hand store with very little wearing in between, they definitely weren't.

Fortunately for all of us and our bank accounts, our husbands declared that they hated this store and did not want to enter it ever again, and because our traveling and gas expenses were so limited, we no longer made the day-long outing.

Outlet stores are a big deal, I know. Every two or three years I forget why I never buy anything there and show up at one of the malls, then after hours wandering around not particularly finding anything, I leave. The same price tags of my and my girlfriend's youth are there -- the original price, crossed out and replaced by the deeply discounted price. But often, if you ignore the Suggested Retail Price (and it's questionable whether anyone, anywhere, ever actually pays this price) and just look at the item, you begin to ask yourself whether it's even worth the discounted price. If you didn't have the illusion that this item were worth four times what is being charged, would you buy it?

When you buy clothes, do two things:

1) Take the piece off of the rack and turn it inside out. Look at the seams and the workmanship -- and while it's easier if you know something about sewing and how clothes are put together, the more you do this, the better you'll get at it.

Check especially the areas of stress that tend to tear out -- under the armpits, in a shirt; in the crotch, in a pair of pants. Does it look like it's holding together? Are there any unraveled seams, loose threads, or even existing gaps in the workmanship?

Now, feel the fabric -- is it thin, flimsy, cheap? Obviously a wool suit jacket is going to be made of sturdier stuff than a t-shirt, but even a t-shirt should feel substantial and as if the fabric has the ability to resist some wear.

Pay no attention to the actual label, unless the company that makes this product is consistently known for the quality and workmanship of its product.

2) If the piece passes this nominal test for workmanship, try it on. Does it fit -- perfectly? Is the color JUST right? Does it look absolutely fabulous on you and you have no misgivings about it *at all*?

If the answer is yes, and you need this item of clothing (or really, really want it and you're treating yourself), then set it aside in the potential purchase pile.

If there is anything at all about the piece that causes you to frown, put it back, no matter how low the price. If it's a bit too tight in the waist, you won't wear it. If it makes your boobs look big but your arms look floppy, you won't wear it. If the color makes your face seem sallow, you won't wear it.

You don't realize this now, in the dressing room when the adrenaline is pumping for you to buy something -- especially something at this incredible price -- but once you're home with the thing and looking for just the right item to wear to that evening's artist reception, you'll pass this piece up. And you'll pass it up next week when you're heading out to dinner. And the week after that at your sister's bridal party.

And you will have spent money -- it doesn't matter how little -- for something that you never wear.

When it comes to clothes, especially, but really to anything that you use on a regular basis -- like a wheat grinder or a set of cooking pots or a leather wallet -- the more you use it, the less you pay, and sometimes it's worth buying less, for more.

For example, I have an alpaca sweater that I knitted, purchasing the yarn for $100. In my mind, $100 is a lot of money, but I justified the purchase because knitting is my hobby, and not only did the $100 represent 5 months worth of indulging myself in that hobby, but the end result was a luxurious sweater -- which would cost a lot more if someone else had knit it, incidentally.

I wear that sweater all the time, and every time I do so, it "costs" a bit less. Like this,

The first time I wore the sweater, it cost $100, not taking into account the whole hobby/knitting thing.

The second time I wore it, it cost me $50 per wear.

The fourth time I wore it, it cost me $25 per wear.

Over the years, I've worn that sweater at least 50 times, and it has many, many more wears left in it yet.

I could have taken the same $100 and bought four sweaters that I really didn't like as much, and that really didn't fit well. If I wound up wearing each sweater twice, each sweater would cost me $12.50 per wear, without anything near the enjoyment I receive every time I put on my alpaca sweater.

When you buy something, if you don't use it, you haven't saved any money, regardless of how little you spent. Do not be fooled by pre-printed price tags that give you a false illusion of a product's true worth by a "before" and "after" price.

(By the way, don't feel bad about it if you have been fooled by these pre-printed price tags. Merchandisers do what they do because these techniques work, like saying $4.99 instead of $5 because most people will round the number down to $4. Once you are aware of a particular practice or technique, you can work your way to not being fooled by it. You can't solve a problem until you realize that it exists in the first place.)

Insurance

Next to property tax, there is no subject that irritates me as much as insurance.

One can argue that insurance, unlike property tax, is not mandatory, to which I pause and say, "Oh really?"

In our state, basic liability auto insurance is mandatory, sort of. That is, if you're an honest person who tries to live decently, you have to buy it, because if you don't, you will be caught and heavily fined. In nearly 70 combined years of driving, Steve and I have never had a parking ticket, much less any sort of infraction or accident -- in my mind, this should result in a practically non-existent insurance premium, but not so. We make up, in our premiums, for those who don't carry liability insurance.

Home owner's insurance isn't mandatory if you don't have a bank loan, like we don't, but if we don't carry it and our house burns down, then the general response will be, "Dumb idiots. You should have had homeowner's insurance." Again, we've never made a claim, and the insurance company rewards us by increasing our premium every year.

Health insurance? The last I heard the Supreme Court declared it a tax and determined that it wasn't unconstitutional to make it mandatory. Of course, the entire system is in flux because none of our elected representatives actually read the healthcare act before they passed it, so surprises will keep showing up. The only surprise that shouldn't surprise us is that those of us who are honest will be charged extra for those who don't pay their premiums, just as with auto insurance.

I sure wish that I could make this a happy chapter and give you all sorts of tips on how to save on your insurance, but this is a large, corporate game run by people who are interested in making money -- yours -- and small, individual people do not have much to say against multi-billion dollar corporations.

That being said, review your insurance purchases and make sure that you're not paying more than you have to. Auto insurance varies widely, and contrary to the warm, funny commercials that you see on TV, some companies are better at making commercials than they are at giving you decent (for insurance companies) premium prices. Our home and auto are insured through a small, regionally owned company that beats the big guys by significant chunk.

With both home and auto insurance, you can reduce your premium by increasing your deductible, the amount that you will pay out of pocket before the insurance kicks in. Since we don't plan to collect on homeowner's insurance unless the house burns down or auto insurance unless the car is totaled, we have a fairly high deductible ($1,000) for each. Because our car is relatively new, we carry comprehensive and collision on it -- again, with a high deductible -- but once the car is more than 10 years old, we'll look into dropping this charge.

Life insurance is something you can be frightened into purchasing more than you need -- we dealt with a reputable financial adviser whom we knew first as a decent human being, and bought enough to cover expenses and keep a roof over the survivor's head if one of us passed on. This was especially important when the children were younger and I, primarily, would have had difficulty making it back into the work world.

Regardless of what you pay in insurance and where, you don't want to be surprised by a six-month premium for your car, or a yearly demand for your house, and not know where to find the money to cover this modern-day necessity expense. Amortize the insurance payment over the months and count this into your budget. While this seems like arcanely basic advice, we knew a couple that, every six months, panicked because the auto insurance was due, and they didn't know how they would pay it. Of course, they could have made monthly payments (which incur a small, but definite "convenience" fee), but they didn't have even those built into their budget. Somehow, every six months, they managed to beg, borrow, or find the amount for the premium, after which they forgot about the need to pay the next one until the next premium check arrived.

As un-fun as this sounds, gather together all the paperwork for your various insurance needs -- auto, home, health, life, rental, business, long term health care -- and look them over to see how you're being charged, and to ensure that you're not paying for something that you don't really need. Make an appointment with the agent who provides you with this product, and go over with him/her what you are purchasing, and see if there are ways that you can save.

If you've got dental or eye care insurance provided through your employer, use it -- Steve's dental insurance which he received when he was working for the company that later downsized him was one of the best things that the company provided. After a yearly $50 deductible, insurance paid for preventive care, and 50-75 percent of any work that needed to be done. Of course, purchasing such insurance for the price that the company paid for it isn't open to us as individuals, and it's more cost effective for us now to take the money that we would pay in premiums and set it aside for dental care. But while he had it -- he used it -- which is something that many people with the same benefit, through their employers, don't do. I know it's no fun to go to the dentist, but it's more fun when much of the bill is being picked up by someone else.

When it comes to insurance in any form, we're reasonably trapped, but keep these bullet points in mind:

- Don't be scared, manipulated, or bullied into buying something you don't need. For example, if you're renting and don't have much in the way of material possessions, you'll pay more in premiums than you will collect should anything happen. No matter how much insurance you buy, in the effort to meet every

53

contingency, life happens, and normal people simply can't afford to insure themselves against everything that could happen. There are ads and commercials and articles that will tell you how miserable your life will be if you need nursing home care and you don't have long term life insurance, but if you're 35 years old with a car payment, a child who needs medication (that isn't covered by your health insurance policy), and a mystery water leak somewhere on your property, you have plenty pulling money out of your paycheck right now. Tune out the fear music and logically look at what you can handle.

- With life insurance, think closely about whom you are insuring. Frequently, after you have a baby, you get all sorts of stuff in the mail about insuring that child as an "investment," but life insurance is pretty much a bet about dying, not about investing money. If you want to set up a financial nest egg for your child, then talk to a trusted financial adviser about doing so, and specifically set up an investment fund.

- Laugh at the cute commercials on TV, but don't believe what they say. Get quotes and look at the numbers. In the same way that you look for a trusted financial adviser, try to find an insurance agent with whom you feel comfortable. We have found success with companies that deal with multiple companies, as opposed to the big conglomerates. In shopping around amongst the smaller, regional companies, our agent has out beat the big guys in price every time, and she's readily available to answer my questions and go over numbers. (And she's accustomed to my outbursts of irritation about premium prices.)

- Make sure that you understand what is being insured, and why you are paying for what you are paying for. Again, this is where having a person you can trust as your agent comes in handy. It's their job to answer your questions, not continue to sell you additional insurance, and you want someone who acts as the mediator between you and the insurance company.

Insurance is a big, complex subject that will not go away unless you find some tropical island to disappear to, and even then, it will follow you. As far as your budget goes, figure out what you're paying; get the numbers down to as low as you can while meeting what you think you need to meet; don't be afraid to ask questions; and don't be fooled by numbers that seem too good to be true. Remember, these people are out to make money, so buy what you have to, but be very very wary about giving your trust along with your money.

Everyone in Our Neighborhood Owns Cows

We live on seven acres outside of a rural town in Southeastern Washington State, and all of our neighbors -- okay, not ALL of them, but a big, hunkin' chunk -- own cows -- some far more than they should on the limited acreage that they have.

Owning cows in Farm Country is considered pretty mandatory, because that's what Country People do -- they own COWS! They eat the MEAT! They take care of THEMSELVES, by gum!

Except for us. We own goats. We also milk the goats, and make lots of cheese. As far as I can see, none of our neighbors milk any of their cows. They just raise 'em. And eat 'em.

But while raising cows, and eating 'em, sounds like a money-saving proposition, it's not as cheap as it seems. One neighbor spends all of his time growing hay, buying the rest, stacking it all, and moving his too-many-cows-for-five acres around the county so that they can eat until it's time to pay the butcher to do his bit, cut and wrap, and call when it's all ready to pick up. Don't even get me started on this neighbor's too-many-pigs-for-five-acres part.

But the meat is fresh and natural, right? Maybe, maybe not -- none of our neighbors are big organic people, so I don't think they're disturbed about the antibiotics in their animal feed.

The point is, everyone owns cows, except for this one odd little family with its three-head goat herd. This is the same odd little family that doesn't use a riding lawn mower to trim the grass, walks our property as opposed to racing around on a Four Track off road vehicle, uses a Walk Behind tractor as opposed to a Big, Real, Looks-like-what-a-farmer-uses model (most plots here are five acres, not 5,000), and gardens. We don't look like Farm Country People; we just look strange.

But we know our land better than many of our neighbors, because we walk on it. During the season, we're out in the garden every day, growing food that we actually eat, because we eat our vegetables, don't just can them and plop them onto the plate next to the day's rump roast. Our goats we milk twice daily, and we see them more than that because we greet one another while they're grazing and we're taking our daily walks for exercise and conversation. Their milk -- which isn't yucky, by the way; goats' milk has an undeservedly bad reputation -- makes a certifiable difference in our grocery bill, and the size of our property well supports three goats, their kids when they have them (those, we eat), and our free range flock of chickens.

We use what we have without abusing over overusing it, and we choose to do things differently from the people around us, because we're doing what fits for us.

This isn't to say that we are right and our neighbors are wrong, but it is an encouragement to customize your lifestyle to what works for you, and not to what your neighbors are doing, or even to what other people in similar situations to yours are doing. If you want a cow, or two, and you're prepared to invest in the infrastructure that you need to keep them, then go for the cows. But if you're like us, and you think -- "A cow's a big, expensive item, and it eats a lot of hay. Goats are smaller, more manageable, and produce just the amount of milk we need. And we don't eat that much meat" -- then get a goat, and don't worry about the snickering.

"But I live in an apartment!"

That's just fine -- lots of people do -- and obviously a goat in the spare bedroom isn't a viable option for you. But this does not mean that you can't homestead -- or have a homesteading attitude -- and save money by doing more for yourself.

As in so many areas of life, the attitude is what matters, and the amount of time we spend lamenting what we *don't* have and what we *can't* do, takes time and energy from our figuring out how to use best what we do have.

"Think outside of the box," we are constantly told, but maybe it would be better to ask ourselves, "Why am I in a box in the first place?"

If you live in a large city, you -- oddly -- may have a viable Farmer's Market set up nearby, and you can purchase fresh produce and farm items for less than I could find them -- and I live in Farm Country. You also have more options for grocery stores, clothing stores, second-hand stores -- wherever you live, you have options that someone who lives somewhere else does not have. Just as they have options that you don't.

Instead of lamenting that you don't live on a 350-acre farm, or a 7-acre farmette, or a big city, or out in the suburbs -- basically any place where you are not, be grateful, first, for having a place to live. Then, look around and see what options are unique to your area, and explore them. If you're not comfortable with the way that most people around you seem to be doing things, then don't feel obligated to join them. You don't have to own cows.

Be aware, however, that owning goats, when everyone else owns cows, requires that you be more resourceful and imaginative, because when something goes wrong, nobody knows how to fix it.

Goats are becoming more fashionable these days (I know, the words "goat" and "fashionable" don't seem to go together, but think, "Cashmere") but in our earliest days of keeping the animals, we could not find a vet that knew what he or she was talking about when we called them out.

Ultimately, what resulted is that we had a lot of dead goats, because other than telling us that the animals had a fever and that they were sick (we had managed to diagnose the situation up to this point), they did little but wish us luck. One time they put the animal down for us, and sent the bill.

As time went by, however, we researched on the Internet, talked to other goat owners, and read our way to a level of competency that resulted in sick goats getting better, because we knew what to do.

This is what you will do with your finances as well. Many of the experts out there, advocating a certain way of doing things ("Make sure to put 15 percent of your take home pay in savings for each child's college education; and don't forget to set aside 25 percent for your retirement") do not have any idea of what it is like to live your life, and it's remarkably easy to dispense advice when you don't have to follow it yourself.

Learn to treat your own goats.

Learn to Cook

Tell me if you've heard this one:

Americans spend less money on food than people in other nations. But they spend more on healthcare.

There's no punch line to this because it's really not a joke.

I know that food costs a lot; I raised a brood of four, and I've spent a lot of time in grocery stores. I spend less time there now, because I've noticed that the longer you're in a store, the more you put into the cart, but I still breathe in sharply every time the clerk announces my total.

But that's okay, any time the total is more than $25, I breathe in sharply.

The point is that yes, food isn't cheap, it isn't getting any cheaper, but we do need it on a regular basis. Manufacturers, knowing that we need to eat, tempt us with all sorts of boxes and cans and frozen products and assorted brightly colored, shouting packages, but even when those products look insanely cheap -- vivid orange macaroni and cheese product comes to mind -- they're really not, in the long run.

If you know how to cook, making macaroni and cheese from scratch takes about as long as making it from the box, but you're able to pronounce all of the ingredients that are in your dinner, and don't be deceived -- chemical additives add up.

I know, I know -- all those unpronounceable ingredients aren't supposed to hurt us at all, and if we suspect that they do, then we're just a bunch of conspiracy minded organic nut cases who think we should weave all of our own clothing out of wool that we've spun from the sheep that we've sheared. And Agent Orange is harmless.

(You will find, as you continue this journey of yours to save money and improve your lifestyle, that you begin to question the motives and motivation of the various people, businesses, and entities in your life who urge you to think a certain way and act accordingly. "Follow the money," is good advice -- to whose advantage is it for you to eat, purchase, or live a certain way? If it's not to yours, then feel free to re-think the process, and reach for a decision that best meets your and your family's needs.)

Our family has decided that the less that was sprayed on our food, inserted into it, swished in the midst of it, sprinkled atop it, or added -- the better off we are. Interestingly, the chefs in this country lead the way in eating fresh, natural food, and the finer restaurants are where you find less processed fare. This is intriguing, coming from people whose highest priorities are taste and presentation.

When you learn to cook, you can replicate the quality of what you eat in a fine restaurant. Granted, you may not produce complex, exotic masterpieces, but if you follow the principle of starting with good, fresh ingredients, you will wind up with something that tastes far, far better than anything you get out of white bag.

As an aside, if you are accustomed to prepared, packaged food, it will be an adjustment switching to the homemade product -- prepared, packaged food has its unique taste often because of the unusual chemical concoction that goes into making it -- but if you accept this and are willing to change, you may soon find that you prefer what you create instead of what is created for you.

It's important to realize that, in the short run as well, packaged food isn't necessarily as cheap as it seems. Not to pick on the color orange, but orange chicken comes to mind -- a favorite food of our middle daughter. In a moment of deliberate mental weakness, I picked up a bag of the prepared product, complete with gorgeous photo on the front of the bag, and convinced myself that it would feed the six of us. After all, the back of the package announced that there were six servings, and if I weren't so desirous of someone else cooking dinner that night, I would have put the bag back after noticing that each serving of rice, chicken, and vegetables consisted of 250 calories.

Even if you're not on a diet, you know that 250 calories for dinner isn't enough. We balanced out the "meal" with apples, toast, cheese, and bananas, and in the amount of time it took to bring the calorie count up, I could have prepared the meal from scratch. AND, I could have pronounced all of the ingredients.

Learning to cook is the single most impacting way that you can reduce your grocery bill, with the added benefit that, once you achieve a nominal level of ability in the matter, everything you eat will taste better than what comes out of a can, box, or bag. Because you focus on buying fewer, better, fresher ingredients, the final product inevitably tastes better than that made from cheaper ingredients made to taste palatable by copious amounts of salt, sugar, fats, and flavor additives.

If you don't cook, or don't cook much, make an effort this week to create one thing from scratch -- and it's okay to use a can of tuna or a bag of noodles or a spice mix. The point is that the finished product -- dinner -- was assembled through your efforts and not through ripping open the box and pulling out envelopes 1, 2, and 3. AND, you can pronounce everything that you're putting into your mouth.

Market Manipulation, Roast Chicken, and You

I don't know about you, but I get vaguely irritated when I realize that I'm being manipulated.

And given the marketing climate in which our society operates, this means that if I don't watch it, I spend two thirds of my day in a vaguely irritated state. The rest of the time I'm sleeping.

The other day I was at the grocery store, humming happily to myself because I was there to pick up a prepared chicken for dinner and would be off the hook for dinner that night. A bright yellow piece of paper with a sickly looking fowl drawn on it announced:

"Four-piece Meal! $2.99!"

Wow. That was $8 off. At that price, I could understand the exclamation points.

And then I read the fine print, which actually wasn't print, but nearly illegible scribble at the bottom of the page:

"With purchase of 10 Happy Mac'n Noodle Ultra-processed Pasta Products in an Envelope at $1 each."

Hmm. A vaguely familiar feeling began creeping through the tissue fiber of my muscles. I stared at the sick chicken, multiplying $1 by 10 and then adding it to $2.99; I came up with $12.99, more than the cost of the dinner I was intending to purchase, but oh! I would also have 10 packages of powdered grain by-product that I really didn't want. For some reason, I felt less consoled than I did that someone was tugging me on my arm, urging me to take advantage of this wondrous, wondrous deal.

Before you point out that I'm being self-righteous here, and that my 8-piece meal is not a sterling example of natural, organic taste and elegance, yeah, I know. I give myself a day off, once a week. This should make you feel better, actually, recognizing that I'm not a purist and certainly don't expect you to be, and that you can be concerned about what you eat on a regular basis without having to be perfect about it. I eat ice cream, too, sometimes when I'm standing over the sink.

You really don't have to feel intimidated by me.

Well, back to the chicken. I don't know how long I stood there, dithering; I'm not sure if my thoughts were audible or not, but I don't think my lips were moving. Eventually, I paid the normal price and walked out without the by-product, on the way passing signs that offered two packs of cookies for every gallon of milk purchased (good thing we milk goats), a jar of jam that would stand up on its own if the jar were removed for three loaves of bread (learn to make your own bread; it's worth it), and a container of salsa with purchase of a Complete Taco Making Kit, complete, that is, except for the meat, lettuce, tomatoes, and sour cream.

Why don't manufacturers offer two bananas for the purchase of 6 apples?

Oh, that's right -- because manufacturers don't make bananas and apples, at least not yet. Actually, that's a good thing. Manufacturers, and large industrial conglomerations, should not be creating our fruits and vegetables. Or patenting their seeds, come to think of it.

But what manufacturers do make are hyper-packaged products that they want to get us to eat, and depend on, and for that reason they'll offer deals that aren't really deals and trick our minds into thinking that we're getting something, when we're really not.

If this irritates you, that's good, because it shows that you recognize you're being manipulated. The happy humming feel resulting from your perspicacity cancels out the irritated feeling at being manipulated, and you walk out of the store in a neutral state.

"SAVE Money on GAS!" a banner across the street proclaims. "10 cents off per gallon (8 gallon maximum) for every 250 Purchase Points Redeemed (1 Purchase Point per gallon of gas)."

Don't you feel better?

Wear Mis-Matched Socks

From the time we are in fourth grade, we pride ourselves on being "different" in this country, and we wear certain clothes, or pierce particular body parts, or color our hair pink, so that we can emphasize how very singular we are from the people around us.

But in many ways, we're scared of being different -- actually different, that is -- truly out of step, no-one-I-know-acts-quite-like-that unusual, which is what you tend to be when your first question is, "Is this truly the best thing for me and my family?" as opposed to, "What will other people say?"

Do you not own a car? That's different.

How about your clothes -- do you wear them two days in a row because they're still clean? That's different. (At the most, in an office situation, which has to be one of the most conforming environments outside of 7th grade gym class, you might be able to wear the same shirt or blouse twice in the same week, but only if it's several days apart.)

Do you wash your dishes by hand because you don't own a dishwasher? Lots of people think that's weird.

Have you ever cut up an old bath towel into squares, serged the edges, and used the smaller pieces as dish rags (with which you hand wash the dishes)? Fairly unusual.

Maybe you don't have a computer, and when you need to use one, you go to the library. You're in the minority there.

If you really want to know how you're different, ask your kids, especially if they're teenagers. They'll probably tell you more than you want to know.

The point is, when you're out to save money and wisely use the resources that come into your household, you will find yourself making decisions that are unique from what your neighbors make, and when you make enough of these decisions, you will start to look out of step from the rest of society.

But that's okay, because most of society spends beyond what it makes and wakes up in the middle of the night, worrying about how to meet next month's charge card statement. Wouldn't you rather be different and not deal with that?

Expect that others will comment on your lifestyle, and rather than meet those comments with downcast eyes and the attitude of a victim ("We just don't have enough money to live like other people"), be proud of who you are and what you're doing.

"Yes, we decided to vacation in our backyard this year," you reply with a smile. "We spent many enjoyable hours around the dining room table planning what we would do, and everyone in the family incorporated a suggestion. It was a truly unusual -- but most gratifyingly different -- experience, and I'm glad we did it."

If you want to practice being different this week, wear mismatched socks. It will be interesting to see if anyone notices in the first place. If they don't, that's a bit of a lesson that sometimes, the things that we think are awkward and obvious, really aren't.

If they do, they may think that you're starting a trend, and that, in a way, you're actually kind of cool. That's another lesson in itself.

And if they do comment on it, and they laugh at you, then it's a good opportunity for you to practice that looking people straight in the eye, smiling, and saying (with aplomb), "Well, so they are. I wonder if I intended to do that, or not?"

The Romance of the Refrigerator

My mother has owned her refrigerator for 45 years. The ice machine still works. Granted, you have to fill it by hand, but as my mother says, "You think I'm going to spend a thousand dollars because I don't want to take five minutes to fill a little container?"

Well, yes, a lot of people do think that way, but not those from my mother's generation, which lived through the Great Depression and knows that a dollar saved today may buy bread tomorrow (or, more accurately, the flour with which to make the bread).

My generation, however, buys a new refrigerator not because the ice machine is broken -- and with the quality of today's appliances versus that which my mother bought 45 years ago, it's highly likely that the ice machine is broken -- but because the new models look nicer, and it's time for something updated and fresh, especially since the microwave was replaced with a stainless steel model last year and the white refrigerator no longer matches.

(My mother's refrigerator is white; the stovetop is black; and the oven is brown.)

Face it -- the old refrigerator is just boring.

Well maybe it is, but the crucial thing is that it works -- which is not something to be taken lightly -- and if you don't need to replace something, especially something utilitarian, then why bother?

Part of the reason why we bother involves the magazines we read and the movies we watch, in which kitchens are beautiful, gleaming, matching things that supposedly ordinary people have as a matter of course, and that we don't shows that we're, well, failures somehow. (Do not underestimate how the constant media environment in which we live affects the way we think and feel -- many times, if you sit down and ask yourself, "Why, really, do I insist upon making this purchase?" you may be surprised at your answer.)

If it weren't for advertisements urging us to replace bland, boxed appliances that are miraculous all in themselves because they wash our clothes, or keep our food warm, or bake our bread, we would keep these items until they were broken. There are far more fun, and utilitarian, ways to spend our money then investing in a matching red, front loading washer and dryer when the white top loaders still work just fine, and if we can't think of something alternative to do with the money, it might not be a bad idea to keep it aside for a day when we truly need to spend it.

Years ago, someone gave us a relatively new refrigerator. It was a cream colored, massively wide and tall, side-by-side double-door monstrosity, and I hated it. It was the wrong color, the wrong size, and it had an ice maker that I wasn't about to pay a plumber to set up. But it was free and it worked, and we were grateful for it.

Well, it almost worked. For some reason, it puddled on the floor -- the incontinent refrigerator, we called it -- and for years we set a bath towel at its base to catch the water that indiscriminately leaked out. Why the water leaked, or where it came from, we never figured out -- although we certainly tried -- but as the refrigerator kept the milk cold and the freezer kept the ice cubes (which we created in little plastic trays) frozen, we regularly replaced the towel and learned to walk around the problem area.

And then, one evening, the refrigerator made a series of gastrointestinal tummy noises, and the next morning, it died. When you live in a rural area 35 miles from the nearest appliance repair shop, which charges $50 just to come out and knock on your door, you think twice about repairing something that is 15 years old and in a terminal state of not working.

So we got online and ordered a refrigerator -- black, which I always wanted, and which cost no more than white -- with one door to the refrigerator on top, and one door to the freezer on the bottom -- also something that I'd always wanted. It wasn't the cheapest model on the block, nor was it the most expensive, but solidly in the middle for a basic box that keeps things cold. We use the same plastic ice tray in the new model that we used in the old.

And we no longer need to put the towel on the floor.

This week, walk through your house, look at your appliances, and be grateful for what it is that they do. Your oven heats up to 500 degrees. Your stove top gets the frying pan hot, and you didn't have to go out and collect sticks in order for it to do so. Your washer accepts the bundle of dirty underwear and gives them back clean. Does it really matter that nothing matches?

Lady, You're Nuts!

Okay, so maybe it's time for one of those concrete, do-this-if-you-want-to-save-money tips that so many books promise. Generally, I avoid bullet-pointed promises or suggestions because they're shallow, don't work if they don't apply to an individual's situation, and get out of hand when you have to come up with ten of them.

(As an aside, I recently traveled to a site promising "10 Ways to Make Money While You're Unemployed" -- I mean, who wouldn't go there with a title like that? One of the top suggestions was to sign up for unemployment benefits. Are you kidding me? Like any person with a pink slip doesn't know that that's an option? Another suggestion was, "Get a part-time job," in which case a person wouldn't be unemployed anymore, and they're probably looking at this article because they're seeking some way, any way, to make money. Anyway, that's why I don't like EZ, cheezie, bullet-point lists of how to solve all your problems.)

So my suggestion for this week? Drop pop, if you drink it. Soda, sodie, whatever you call a carbonated artificially flavored drink -- stop drinking it.

Even when you buy it on sale, it's not cheap replacing water -- which is sort of free if you don't mind drinking out of the tap -- with whatever the purchase price is every time you take a drink. We know people who put the stuff on the dinner table for the meal's beverage; health issues aside, that's a financial drain for a product that provides no nutrients, no vitamins, no fiber, no food value. The amount you pay for a regular monthly supply of carbonated beverage could pick up extra bananas, a good cut of grass fed beef, real butter, some decent yogurt. The exchange is a good one.

And regarding those health issues -- if you drink the stuff with sugar, you shouldn't be surprised that there will be weight gain, dental caries, and that feeling of general lassitude that an overdose of sugar can produce (or, in some people, that bouncing off the walls sensation). If you drink the stuff laced with artificial sweeteners, well, you're pumping a lot of unknown, chemical additives unnecessarily into your system -- do you really want to do that?

So what do you drink instead? Try water. And if you get on me about the necessity of purchasing bottled water because municipal tap water isn't safe or healthy, you're drinking pop, aren't you? Get past that first, then worry about the water. Just get over the pop.

We drink a lot of tea -- hot or cold -- which we purchase as bulk leaves from Upton Tea Imports based in Massachusetts. Because tea is a heavily sprayed product, we buy organic when we can, and we make several pots from the morning's leaves. By evening, we mix the highly weakened mixture with half milk and spices to create a comforting Chai mixture; generally, we get three or four steepings out of several tablespoons of leaves. Tea has a lot of antioxidant and health benefits, so even though it doesn't provide calorie nutrients, it's full of potential health improving properties. (The Ultimate Tea Diet by Mark Ukra is a good read on tea.)

But water always works. On the rare occasions when we eat at a restaurant (because we know how to cook, and cook well, remember), we never order a beverage, because the funds we have allotted will go further buying good food if we don't pay the overpriced amount for pop, milk, wine, coffee, or even tea (which generally arrives as a mug of hot water and a tea bag -- that is one expensive tea bag).

So, this week, if you drink pop, drop it. Altogether would be nice, so you're not tempted at all, but even cutting down will make a difference. Some people are more tempted by pop than others, and dropping or reducing it will be a challenge, but it's a challenge worth taking on.

Mankind has survived without this stuff for many, many centuries, and though it may be difficult, you can too. This is one small, completely superfluous purchase that you can remove from your weekly budget -- and if there are enough of you in the household carting home cases and dropping in at the Quick Stop for a Big Man's Thirst Quencher -- you will rapidly see an increase in available change.

(As an interesting aside, we make Kombucha, a fermented tea that some people say reminds them of pop that they have drunk overseas. At its best, it's fizzy, mildly sweet with a tang, and extremely refreshing on a cold day. It's also remarkably easy to make, and incredibly expensive to buy -- so if you're feeling experimental, look up Kombucha recipes on the Internet and see if it's something that you want to try. Kombucha is high in what is called probiotics, the "good" bacteria that is supposed to be beneficial to our digestive system, and which many of us don't get enough of.

The other day I was looking through a coupon book and found ads for all sorts of Power Probiotics in Pill Form -- every few years we get another fad to follow, and I guess Anti-oxidants have had their moment in the sun. The main point is, you can buy all of this stuff, or you can figure out how to get it in your food or drink, and when you do the latter, you save money as well empower yourself.

Learn to cook. I'm sure I've said that before.)

Take a Serious Look at Your Garbage Can

Just recently, we've dropped garbage service from once a week to once a month, because we found that it took great effort to fill a 96-gallon container every Tuesday. More than one Wednesday at 6 a.m. we heard the chuggy chuggy sound of the disposal truck and thought,

"Oops! We forgot to put out the can. Guess we'll have to remember next week."

After enough times of not remembering the next week, either, it occurred to us that we didn't generate a lot of garbage. Around the same time, we actually read the newsletter insert from the disposal company and noticed that they offered a once a month option. Not only that, but they charged a quarter of the amount as they did for weekly service, which only makes sense to most of us, but when you're talking about public utility companies, making sense is not a top priority.

This chapter isn't so much about seeing if your disposal company is sensible or not as it is about the amount of consumer waste you generate, and what this says about your spending habits:

The more you buy, the more garbage you will generate, whether you put the waste products in your garbage can, recycle bin, woodstove, or compost pile.

Now there's not much you can do about the daily junk mail deluge -- that comes to your home, free of charge, whether you want it or not. If you are receiving a lot of catalogs, however, you might want to stop and look at them, not so much to buy as to identify if you are purchasing so much that you're on a regular list. The catalogs you receive say something about your spending habits.

We get a few catalogs -- mainly garden seed companies and die-hard clothing outlets that are convinced that, because we make one purchase every 15 months or so, we're worth pursuing. If you get a regular stack, however -- clothing, garden supplies, kitchen equipment, digital toys, books, novelty foods, furniture, office supplies, pet products -- keep them to the side for a month and get a visual of where your money goes, or has gone.

Now, as to the rest of your garbage can: what is filling it up?

I know from visiting my college-aged daughter and her roommates that pizza boxes and pop cans fill a plastic receptacle quickly, and it doesn't count to say, "Oh, but that's the recycling bin!" It's still garbage, representing something that you purchased, used, and threw away.

If your garbage can and recycling bins are filling quickly, then it's because you're stuffing them full of packaging, and packaged items are expensive. It's highly unlikely that most people's garbage cans are getting full from fruit peels and vegetable waste (which make great compost, if you've got any yard at all). Plastic liter pop bottles, macaroni and cheese boxes, dried cereal containers, TV dinners or family-sized prepared meals, bubble wrap and styrofoam peanuts from online purchases, not to mention the plastic wrapping -- impossible to remove without a knife -- that encases digital media and toys -- take up a lot of room in the garbage can.

While you don't necessarily have to put on plastic gloves and poke through the egg shells and coffee grounds, do be aware of what you're tossing away, and how it represents what you purchased. The less you buy that is packaged, food or not, the less you will put in the garbage can.

Let's see if I can put this delicately, in case you're one of those people who likes to read while you're eating lunch:

Waste products say a lot about a person. While it's true that hypochondriacs are overly concerned about their bathroom activity, anybody going through health issues is aware of what their body is processing and how.

In the same way, your household is a living organism, taking things in, and spewing things out. What it spews out, and how much of it, says a lot about what is going in. The less going in -- purchases, especially those with packaging -- the less coming out.

It's like counting calories when you're dieting -- you don't so much have to write down numbers after every meal or snack as you watch what's coming in -- is it an apple or a candy bar? The former will have more nutrition per calorie than the latter, and it is a better food choice. Rather than remember all sorts of numbers about protein content and fat calories versus carbohydrates, I just focus on high fiber versus low, recognizing that with the former, I get more for less.

So it is with consumer products -- is it a flour bag representing the raw ingredients you used to make your own crackers? Or is it the box from the ready-made, processed, and not inexpensive crackers? The flour bag represents enough raw ingredients to make many, many boxes of crackers, and it takes up far less space in your garbage can.

This week, be aware of what goes in the garbage. You don't have to be odd about this; just observe. Keep track of how many times you empty the household wastebaskets, and be aware, especially aware, if you have to jump on top of the garbage can lid in order to keep it from popping open.

As with any of the changes and adjustments you are making in your life and lifestyle to save money, don't beat yourself up about this, tearing yourself apart because you generate too much garbage. Think of this as a game -- an intriguing challenge -- constantly thinking of new ways or means by which you decrease the amount of packaging in your life.

Take Care of Your Teeth

Dental care is expensive, and many of us do not have dental insurance.

That being said, not getting basic dental care winds up being more expensive in the long run, and if you can find a way to make a cleaning and check up appointment at least once a year, you will thank yourself 20 years from now.

At one point in our family, we had four dentists -- The Norwegian Artist, when he still worked in cubicle world, had decent dental insurance through his employer, so he was able to go to the dentist of his choice. The kids had different dentists who took state-provided dental benefits -- something we were eligible for even while the Norwegian worked full time, which says a lot about how much the business community is willing to pay its cadre of white collar workers. I landed in a low-cost community clinic -- I am fortunate in that I've had the same amazing hygienist for more than 20 years, but the dentists are a rotating array of students just out of school, working off their loans. Some are good. Some aren't.

But the crucial thing is that all of us keep our teeth looked at and cared for on a regular basis, and not so much time goes by that a small problem grows large. The plaque is removed, small cavities filled, the mouth emerges clean.

One of our relatives provided an annual trip to the dentist to her daughter as the yearly birthday present. I found this out when the daughter landed a job, with benefits, and I joked, "Now you can go to the dentist and get everything taken care of."

"It already is," she replied. "That annual trip to the dentist may not seem like an exciting or fun birthday present, but it's one I'm really grateful for. I never had to have dreams at night about my teeth falling out because they were rotting away."

Along with that annual checkup is daily, regular care of your teeth. Brush and floss every day -- surely that sounds like something your mother said? Well, she was right, and a regular habit of cleaning our teeth, daily, increases the likelihood of a good report at the dentist's later.

The amount you spend in floss, toothbrushes, and toothpaste (if you use it) is negligible, and the amount of time it takes to regularly use these products eventually seems like nothing when you make it an incontrovertible part of your daily routine. We use Sonicare electric toothbrushes, which one of our dentists sold to us for a wholesale price, and the positive results made up for their purchase. But even a 99 cent toothbrush from the discount outlet store is a powerful tool when it's actually used.

If you've ever had a toothache, or needed a root canal, you'll appreciate that a healthy mouth that you know is well cared for, is worth a lot. Put aside money for your dental care.

(And by the way, it's not an accident that this chapter follows so closely after the one about dropping pop. Quit soaking your teeth with sugar water, and you'll go a long way toward keeping your mouth happy.)

Take Care of Your Car

While we're talking about taking care of things, take care of your car, and if you don't already have a plan for making regular oil changes, rotating the tires, and getting the overall vehicle looked at, build one in.

If your car is newer, it may handle of a lot of this mental record work for you. Two years ago, for the first time in our lives, we purchased a new car for which we had been setting aside money for years. One of the features of our Honda Fit is that you press a little button on the dashboard and it tells you when the oil needs to be changed. Along with each oil change is a manufacturer's recommended schedule of maintenance, and we budget it in just as we do care for our teeth.

(Oil changes in newer cars tend to be spread out longer than those of older cars -- our Fit demands a change every 7,500 to 10,000 miles; our 1990 Buick, may it rest in peace, went in every 2,000 - 3,000 miles; find out your magic number and stick with it -- if you don't see the importance of this, the next time you get your oil changed, ask to look at the dirty oil they're draining out. Think about that stuff flowing through your engine.)

Our older cars -- when we had them -- had no such buttons and levers, and we worked closely with our mechanic to ensure that the necessary maintenance was done at the right time.

Speaking of mechanics, since you will be relying upon one so heavily, make sure that you trust yours. I know, mechanics are like used car salesman -- we are convinced that they're out to cheat us -- and some of them are, just as there are people out to cheat us in any profession or industry.

Rather than disbelieve everything your mechanic says, ask around, search around, and find a mechanic and shop that you can rely upon for its honesty, integrity, and skill. The time you spend finding this person will pay back by 1) your increased peace of mind that what you're told is valid, and 2) the better care your car will receive because you're giving it what the expert says it needs.

We have found success with shops that are ASE (Automotive Service Excellence) accredited. The ASE is a non-profit institute that reviews professionals in the automotive repair industry for their expertise and quality, and the ASE logo outside the shop is a good thing to look for.

I have found least success, especially as a woman who looks like she doesn't know anything about cars (I don't) at Cheap Oil Change chain shops, as well as at some regional and national franchised outfits that assure me how much they care about me, but spend a lot of time convincing me to purchase this product and that. In no time at all, my $29.95 promised oil change has quadrupled in price.

Years ago, I had just had my car at my mechanic's, and it was due for an oil change, which, unfortunately, this mechanic did not do. Knowing where I was going the next day, however, he took a quick look under the hood and pulled out the air filter.

"They're going to tell you that you need a new one of these," he warned me. "This one's fine for another go -- just tell them to blow the dust out."

Sure enough, the next day, the technician appeared like a wraith, air filter cradled in his hands

"Ma'am, you need a new one of these." His voice was soft, gentle, sepulchral.

"Blow it out, please."

Upshot of this chapter: Maintain your car and find a mechanic you can trust.

Buy Basic

Let's not leave the concepts of cars just yet.

I don't know where you are in your life right now -- if you're wanting to save money because you've still got a job, or two, but find things aren't stretching as far as they used to, or if you're in survival mode because you're out of a job and you're trying to keep food on the table.

If you're in the latter category, you're probably not in the market for a car, but when the day comes that you look for one, here are some things to keep in mind.

As I mentioned in the last chapter, we have bought one new car in our lives, this after 28 years of marriage, and that only because we couldn't find a used car for a decent price that would deliver the mileage, reliability, and most importantly -- superlative space for transporting things, in our case, fine art paintings.

As you can see, we had a criteria list:

- Good gas mileage
- Decent price
- Solid record of quality
- Space for transporting items

You'll notice that the cool factor does not come into play on this list, and if you want to save money on a car -- new or used -- please try to get over strongly associating who you are with what you drive.

I know this is hard -- car advertisements are not particularly subtle, and after watching them you know very little about the product itself, but you do have this feeling that if you buy it, you will be happy, sexy, dashing, popular, and able to drive 100 miles an hour over windy, yet smooth roads that lead to the top of mesas or cliffs.

When I first scouted out car options before our Honda Fit purchase, I walked into the automobile dealership, shook hands with the sales associate, and said,

"I want a car with good gas mileage, in this price range, that is known for lasting a long time, and that has a lot of space. I don't know what mag wheels are, so I don't care if it has them. Hubcaps don't enter my awareness zones unless they're loose. I do not measure my self-esteem by my car, but I do place great importance upon owning a car I can rely on."

After his initial surprise, he nodded and said, "I've got just the thing for you."

And he did, but of course I didn't buy it just then because this was a reconnaissance trip, but I took his card so that I could purchase it from him if, after my researching the price, I found that he could give me the best deal.

Unfortunately, he couldn't, but somebody else three-hours away was willing to work with me, and we came to an equitable purchase price. Steve and I did our homework regarding the price ranges our auto of choice came in, and when we wrote the check (remember, we had been saving money aside for years), we were confident that we were getting a decent deal.

You are more than your car, and you will find more money in your pocket or bank account if you accept that automobiles are amazing tools that get us places quickly, but they are not an extension of our personality or a sign to the world that we are successful, sexy, and smart.

Smart Phones Aren't Necessarily Smart Buys

One chapter segues into another. We left the last essay with an admonition that what we drive is not a symbol of who we are. Phones fall into the same category.

For years, we resisted getting a cell phone because 1) we didn't need one, 2) we live in a rural area that doesn't get good service, and 3) we found the convoluted, expensive, and deliberately confusing "plans" to be manipulative and financially unsound.

In the same way that we do not define ourselves by what we drive, we don't consider ourselves James Bond cool because we hold a flat, black quadrilateral against our ear and talk into it. Or worse, press buttons and run our fingers over the screen, checking Facebook because we can't exist without seeing how many people Liked our latest post.

And regarding the GPS app -- The Norwegian Artist and I both know how to read a map, which doesn't scold us in a British voice, nor direct us to the middle of a wheat field and tell us that we have reached our destination.

We spend a lot of money in this country on small, electronic gadgets, and frequently we are less concerned about what they do than by how we look using them. When you think about it, the primary purpose behind a phone is to, well, make phone calls, or send texts -- to communicate, essentially, and if a cheap model from a box store -- the kind that you load with minutes every month -- performs this function, then it doesn't matter whether it speaks to you in a clipped British accent as it leaves you in the middle of the field.

"This phone is six months old," someone told me once. "People are looking at me like I'm too poor to replace it or something."

This is a really bad reason, financially, intellectually, or emotionally, to buy a product, and if you are always chasing after the latest gadget, you will always be spending money. As with anything, we can convince ourselves that we need a certain product; in the case of the phone, we are attracted to all the things it does in addition to making phone calls -- we can watch movies on it, or shop, or keep intricate lists -- and if we really do all these things, then perhaps we're getting our money's worth. But if our phones do the same things that our Netbooks do, and our Netbooks replicate what our laptop does, and our laptop is a portable version of our computer -- we are investing in a lot of electronic gadgetry, and electronic gadgetry is not cheap.

Also, the more electronics that we have in our life, the less of a life we have, in a certain sense. We are never away, never out of reach, never alone and unable to be called, texted, pinged, buzzed, or nudged. There is something to be said of solitude and silence, and we truly need time with each of these every day.

Stepping back is always a good idea. The more that we are absorbed in a particular arena -- like electronic phone gadgetry -- the less likely that we are to think objectively. When we're constantly playing with our phone, constantly comparing that phone to the products of the people around us, constantly being barraged by commercials haranguing us into updating that phone, and *intrinsically identifying our self worth* by that phone -- the more vulnerable we are, financially, to catapulting, and buying something we basically already have, but just in another shape, size, or color.

Rise above your phone.

Not Everyone Is out to Cheat You

So we've talked about mechanics, and used car salesman, and phone companies. There's a general belief in this country that people are out to cheat us, and like many general beliefs, it's there for a reason.

Because, actually, many people are out there to cheat us. The most recent scam call that came through this afternoon comes to mind, the one with the tape recorded message on the other end telling me that they've tried to reach me three times, and they will be sending out the sheriff soon to collect the money I owe.

Only, I don't owe anybody any money.

Daily, our senses are barraged by pop-up screen ads, books that promise an *EZ Million in 10 Days (If You're Smart)*, subtle manipulation techniques leading us through certain aisles of the grocery store, television advertisements that are big on emotion but small on facts, newspaper articles that prod us into thinking a certain way -- it goes on and on, the people and businesses and establishments that are out to get as much money as they can out of us, while delivering less than what they appear to promise.

But there's one group of people that isn't the problem, and it's the one group we attack with vehemence, convinced that they're charging us too much, and by God, we're going to barter them down until we pay the price we ought to be paying -- small business owners, specifically, people who create or grow items for sale.

The Norwegian Artist and I are such small business owners -- Steve creates fine art paintings that we sell as originals, signed limited edition prints, and posters -- all of which we price reasonably, considering Steve's skill and what we are offering. And yet, there are those people who think we're just there to fleece them -- I recall a client once who was looking at a $400 painting and wanted to know, "How much will you take off if I don't take the frame?"

Well you know, the frame is there as a courtesy. I'm sorry you don't like it. But we took off $50 (I'm laying a bet the client was ready to spend three times that on the replacement frame; people do that -- they want the artwork for $50 and they'll go to a frame shop and drop $250 for the frame job).

"What about tax? Is that $350 with tax included?"

Are you kidding? I know where this guy was staying that night -- a hotel for $175 -- and dinner would be another $100 after he paid $35 for a bottle of wine he could pick up at the grocery for $15.

And he went on, and on, and on, convinced that we were making massive amounts of money off of savvy, smart people like him.

We're not out to cheat people. We provide something that most people can't even dream of creating on their own -- a fine art oil painting -- and in order to continue doing so, we really do need to eat now and then. What Steve does is no less skilled than your dentist or orthodontist or mechanic or plastic surgeon or computer repair technician -- and people don't barter with them.

But oh, the poor person at the Farmer's Market trying to sell you some zucchini.

"That's more than I'd pay at the store."

Well maybe it is, but it hasn't been to Antarctica and back, shipped from one warehouse to the next, and raised in an agribusiness field that looks like a desert when it doesn't have plants on it, and the money for that little zucchini enables an individual to make a living outside of an office cubicle.

The guy who owns the toy store on Main Street doesn't charge more than the box store because he's greedy. And while people wouldn't dream of chasing down the manager of the box store and demanding a reduction in price, they have no problem approaching the individual business owner.

Yes, people are out to cheat you, and to keep a rein on your finances, you need to figure out who they are and sidestep their tricks and manipulations.

But they're not the small guys.

We have a tendency in this country to judge our financial acumen by whether or not we pay retail, and purchasing a $100 item for $25 is always a sign of a crafty, cunning, clever person.

If you think about it, though, "crafty," "cunning," and "clever," while they do describe a person's intelligence, don't say much for his integrity and honesty, and if you're always concerned that you're being ripped off, consider doing two things:

1) Find someone you trust to do business with and do business with them. We work with a contractor who is as straight as the level he uses, and if he says something will cost this much, then it costs this much. I wouldn't insult him by telling him to offer a lower price.

2) Worry less about the dishonesty of other people and focus on the honesty in your own life. Yes, there are slimy, creepy people out there, and they're really good at looking genuine and sincere. But the more genuine and sincere that you become yourself, the more readily you will identify the falseness in someone else. It's one of those gut feeling, instinctive things that grows as you do.

You'll still get tricked, now and then, but it's better to be tricked now and then than to go through life thinking EVERYONE is a slime.

Don't Be Scammed

Slimy, repulsive, wriggling lizards are out there everywhere, and yes, I know that most lizards aren't slimy. So these people have dry, scaly, flakey, peeling skin.

No matter how private you try to keep your life, Big Brother's watching you on one side and his cousins in the marketing department are keeping records on the other side, and the information gathered finds itself into the hands of more cousins and second cousins and your sister-in-law's nephew's son's best friend. And you get phone calls and e-mails and letters from all sorts of official looking places and people, telling you that you owe money and they're ready to serve a warrant on you, or they need your bank account number to fix a little glitch in their information system, or they want to know your mom's maiden name because they're sure that they went to school with her years ago.

Oh, and let's not forget your aunt, who has never been outside of the state, contacting you via Facebook to let you know that she's stranded in Bangladesh and she needs some money for the plane ticket back.

This is a good time to learn how to use the word, "No," and to practice not doing what others expect, urge, and pressure you into doing.

If you get a phone call that you weren't expecting, and the person on the other end claims to be from your bank, the local police force, the school, a business you frequent -- and they're asking you personal information -- try this sentence:

"I didn't generate this call, and while I'd like to help you if you are legitimate, I do not respond to unsolicited communication. I will hang up and call you at the place from which your purport to be."

(If you don't want to use the word "purport," that's okay, but it makes you sound really intellectual.)

Then, if you feel that what they've told you is something you need to follow up on, look up the genuine number of the business from which they purport to be, call it, and see if someone is actually trying to get hold of you.

More often, however, you get a call from a number you don't recognize, generating from a geographical region in which you don't live, and they tell you that your credit card is having problem, or you are overdrawn at the bank, or someone is suing you. Hang up. Just hang up.

Then type the phone number (if you've got Caller ID, and if I've got it, you've probably got it) into the Internet search engine and see what comes up. Most of the time you'll get something along the lines of, "Did you get a call from XXX-YYY-ZZZZ? These people call all the time and tell me that I owe money."

99

A legitimate organization trying to reach you for legal or business reasons is not going to simply call you on the phone, and if they do, they will give you complete information as to who and what they are -- enough so that you can look them up on the Internet or in the phone book and actually find them.

Other times, the scams are in your e-mail inbox -- again, purporting to be from your bank, or your credit card company, or the IRS, or your local office supply store. Many times, the return e-mail addresses of these messages look funny, along the lines of 12ydjj59xs@email.com, but by the time you're reading this, the lizards could have improved on that.

As with a phone call, be suspicious of any unsolicited communication that demands something of you -- personal information, money, the insistence that you call their toll-free number and speak to one of their operators. Think twice -- three or four times -- before you click on any links or reply to these e-mails. If the message appears to be from a business with which you do, indeed, do regular business, either get on the phone and call the place, or look up its legitimate e-mail address and write them.

Be vigilant. Be wary. Be willing to say, "No, I'm not going to do that right now."

In one of the earliest scam phone calls I took, before I realized how many of these operations are out there, I had the presence of mind to ask, "Who is demanding this action of me?"

"Ma'am, you need to call this number I'm going to give you," the operator was firm and insistent.

"But who are these people? Whom do you represent?"

"Ma'am, as soon as you get off the phone, you need to call this phone number."

"As soon as I get off this phone, I'm calling the sheriff's office."

Click.

Since the beginning of time, there have always been people who have chosen to use their brains and ability and cleverness to cheat others. While you don't have to be paranoid, keep up on things; the easiest way is to type Latest Scams into the Internet and read what comes up. It's pretty interesting, and, unfortunately, ever changing and evolving.

Be assured that, whatever new technology comes into our lives, dishonest people will find a means to use it to line their own pockets with money, which I sincerely hope does not come from my bank account or yours. Knowledge is power, as they say.

Impulse Buying versus a Wise Investment

Sometimes the best pieces of advice don't seem real because they don't seem like advice.

Like this one:

Wait, before you make a purchase.

See what I mean? It's so prosaic, so basic, so sensible that it's almost boring, and it's tempting to pass on it as you head through the store aisles tossing stuff into the cart.

"Oh look -- a set of three cordless phones, one with answering machine, for an eminently reasonable price. A really, really reasonable price."

Of course, you already have a set of four cordless phones, one with an answering machine, and they're working just fine.

"But it's an eminently, eminently reasonable price. And three is actually better than four -- simpler, actually -- and it won't be this price forever. And I like the color."

Ah. There's the rub. If they looked exactly like the phones you have now, only three instead of four, would you be so determined to buy them?

Why not go home and wait on it for a day or two? They'll probably be the same price on Tuesday.

I mention phones specifically because I was looking for a set -- two out of four of my cordless phones are in a state of, well, not working -- and my favorite warehouse store had a set of three for an eminently, eminently reasonable price. But the main thing I was hoping for was a phone into which I could plug my headphones, so that I can use my hands while I talk -- if only to gesticulate wildly in the air, as this mysteriously advances my thought process -- and this box of phones, which look just like the phones I have right now, didn't deliver.

So I decided to wait. Given that some phone -- four-pack, three-pack, two-pack -- is always on sale at this store, I know that I can find a replacement when the remaining two handsets die, and physically removing myself from the product's box was like walking out of the bakery; the cheesecake's siren call wafted away on the wind.

It's two weeks later; my two phones still work; and the eminently reasonable amount of money that the phones would have cost me is still in my bank account; I can buy something fun with it, like extra electricity to run the lights for the month, or maybe I'll lower the deductible on my car insurance. There's always something.

And that's the point -- spending money in this country is easy because so many people are demanding it, and some of them you can't refuse -- it's nearly time for our twice annual rent payment to the king, er, state, for the privilege of living in the house that we own, and this is not one of those "purchases" that I can wait on and see if I want to make, because, frankly, I would never want to make it.

But those other purchases -- those impulse buys that masquerade as solid investments because they are so eminently, eminently reasonably priced -- can wait a day or two as I see how life goes on without them.

And then, when I do save money by not purchasing something I don't really need or want, I set as much as I can aside for the real things -- the items that give me pleasure and enjoyment and contentment and encouragement, the ones about which years later I say, "I'm so glad I bought that. I use it/see it/enjoy it every day."

That's not impulse buying. That's a wise investment.

Turn off the Lights!

Saving money is a combination of big chunks -- like refinancing your house loan to a lower interest to save a significant amount each month -- and little bits and pieces. You'll be surprised at how those little bits and pieces add up.

Which brings us to the electric bill and the standard parental emission that just drops off our lips without our even thinking about it:

"Who was last in the bathroom? Turn off the lights!"

"Is anyone in this kitchen? Then why are the lights on?"

"You don't need lights on in the hallway in the middle of the day. Turn them off!"

Are you seeing a theme here?

Given how often lights are left on throughout a house, you'd think that there was something extraordinarily difficult about pressing the switch downward, but really, it's just as easy to turn the lights on as it is off. And even with the compact fluorescent light bulbs (which are great, I agree, in that they don't use as much electricity, but they do, um, have mercury in them, and mercury isn't something you just toss in your kitchen garbage can. But people will), you still don't want to pay -- anything -- for lighting rooms that you're not in.

So if you're the problem, train yourself to turn the lights off when you leave the room.

If it's your kids, then train them, and this means that you'll sound like an unpopular nag for awhile, but what parent doesn't?

Rather than follow them around, muttering, and turning the lights off behind them, encourage them to accept responsibility for their actions. This is what it looks like at our house:

We're at the dining room table, and I see that the bathroom light is on.

Me: "Who was last in the bathroom?"

Tired of Being Youngest: "Me."

Me: "Then before you start eating, will you please turn off the light?"

If you can't get anyone to admit to it, then choose a child, any child (you probably know the culprit), and ask them to turn off the light before eating cookies, watching a movie, knitting a sock, or whatever it is that they're planning to do. If you get the, "But it wasn't me!" ignore the grammatical mistake and focus on the issue,

"Maybe not, but it definitely wasn't I. And since you've had your share of leaving the lights on in the past, it won't hurt you to turn this one off. It'll make up for one of the times that I turned a light off after you."

Not that long ago, College Girl was living in a house with five other people, and she lamented at the amount of the electricity bill.

"They leave lights on EVERYWHERE!" she exclaimed. "I spend all day walking through the rooms, announcing loudly, 'Let's turn those lights off when we don't need them, okay?'

"I feel like I'm you."

So yes, one little light left on isn't such a big deal, but it doesn't take long for five lights to be left on, and if there are enough people in your household, you can quickly reach 10 or 20 lights left on in unoccupied rooms, and that adds up. Maybe it's nickels and dimes and quarters, but do you toss a quarter in the parking lot every time you go grocery shopping?

What Is a Basic Utility?

Let's not leave the subject of utilities just yet.

Generally, we think of utilities as those little basics that make life easier, which are difficult to provide for ourselves individually: water, electricity, a means of heating our home, garbage, and the telephone come immediately to mind.

Now while you can get by without, say, the telephone, it is a bit difficult, and I speak from experience. In our first year of marriage, wretchedly poor financially but not otherwise, we forewent telephone service much to the frustration and angst of our parents, who could only get a hold of us by calling a neighbor or our place of work. We, also, found the lack of phone communication isolating, although we never did have to worry about telemarketing or scam callers during dinner.

So I list telephone service as a sort of basic necessity that's worth having, along with Internet service. This latter is essential to us, since we run an online art gallery and I write for numerous online publications. For people like my parents, however, who still use a rotary phone, Internet just isn't a necessity, so they don't incur that monthly bill.

You, also, will look through your life and see what utility services are necessary. Take air conditioning, for instance, which isn't so much a utility in itself as a product that uses a utility, mainly electricity.

We have no air conditioner.

"But you live in the Pacific Northwest where it rains all the time," you point out.

Well, sort of. While we do live in the Pacific Northwest, the region does encompass more than the city of Seattle, and we live on the east side of the Cascade Mountains, where it is dry, and, in the summer, easily able to reach over 100 degrees and stay there.

It. Gets. Hot.

But only for two months out of the year, and sometimes it cools down to 80 at night.

So we just slow down during July and August, and don't live as if it were May or October -- kind of like the rest of the world, in the tropics, where entire cultures revolve around taking breaks in the afternoon and continuing life further into the evening, when the temperature goes down. Of course, in many places, these entire cultures are adapting and changing to look more like the American way, as more and more people acquire air conditioners.

Our daughter, in Tucson, AZ, went through her entire first summer season there without clicking on the air conditioner, primarily because -- as a college student -- she is chronically short on money, but also because she has accustomed her body to work around the heat. It's not that she doesn't enjoy an air conditioned room; it's just that she doesn't want the money that could go for groceries be spent on utilities. So she adapts. She mentioned that this year, because money isn't so tight, she may consider turning on the air conditioner now and again, but then again, she may not.

A couple years ago, when unemployment was all the rage (actually, I think it's a permanent part of our new, improved, global economy), I remember reading one of those non-news-human-feature articles in which a woman commented,

"I don't know how I can live on the amount that unemployment will pay. How will I meet my cable TV bill?"

At this point, my interest in this human interest story plummeted to zero.

Just when did cable TV become a basic necessity like electricity or potable water?

Not all utilities are created equal, and you may find that you can eliminate one -- like cable TV -- or decrease the amount you use another -- like electricity, by moderating your air conditioning use or decreasing the amount you use your clothes dryer (which consume a lot of energy, by the way) by hanging your clothes up on a rack or outside. It's really not that weird.

Water usage is another area that can suck you dry, so to speak. Many municipalities permit you a base amount; interestingly, this amount is frequently not represented in gallons per month usage, something that the average person can understand and work around. Rather, there is some complex formula involving equations and six digit numbers -- I spent an appreciable time with the city clerk once trying to figure out just how much water we were permitted to use before they dinged us for "extra usage," and I never did get the numbers down.

But what I do know is that we stay under the minimum, and that most people don't. Even when there were six of us in the family, we stayed under the minimum, because the back of my mind was always listening for a toilet running, or someone rinsing dishes under a running tap, or a shower that went on and on and on. During the summer, we are fortunate to have water rights so that we can irrigate our property and garden from the river, but don't get too excited about that, because what we save in water fees, the electric company makes up in their own "over-usage" charges.

One year, our oldest daughter and her then-boyfriend watched our house while we were on a two-week vacation, and next month's water bill was a shocker -- nearly twice the base amount. It didn't take long to figure out that the boyfriend, a confirmed narcissist, enjoyed 45-minute showers, which not only negatively impacted our water bill, but our propane tank -- which heats the water -- as well.

So as I mentioned in the article about turning off the lights, it's the little things you do, or don't do, each day that add up and make a difference. Consider that, in most of the world, people do not have cheap, reliable electricity; potable water from the tap; or multiple large screen televisions, surround sound systems, and computer networks. They learn to live with what they have, and necessity dictates that they don't waste or overuse.

- Consider washing your dishes by hand, and doing so once or twice a day. Just because your household

111

has more than one person in it doesn't mean that this is an impossible feat -- children and chores are a great combination, as I will address in the chapter, You Don't Have to Do This All By Yourself, You Know. (Oh, and by the way, there is a huge, ongoing debate about whether you use less water with a dishwasher or washing dishes by hand; although to make it fair, you need to factor in the cost of electricity to run the dishwasher as well as the cost of the appliance itself. It's probably not too hard to figure out my opinion in the debate.)

- Take shorter showers.

- Put on a sweater and keep the heat thermostat a few degrees lower. My Southern California grandmother used to drive my parents to distraction when she shivered in her fine, gauzy, fashionable blouse. "It's snowing outside," my father would point out. "And it's freezing inside," she would snap. (Other than that consistent contention, the visits were well enjoyed and looked forward to. I think my parents began encouraging my grandmother to arrive in the spring or early fall.)

- Turn off the light if there's no one in the room.

- Keep an eye on use, and overuse, and don't take utilities for granted.

- Watch the air conditioner, if you have one. If your health permits and you are not adversely affected by hot weather, challenge yourself to see how long you can keep the air conditioner off by opening windows, using fans, and slapping a cold rag over your head. We know people who have the thing chugging all day and all night, and even when the temperature drops to a bearable 80 degrees, they're so accustomed to the chill factor that they just slip on a sweater and keep the appliance running.

- And, if the funds are low, don't worry about meeting the cable TV bill. It's really not a necessity. Not like potable water.

Make Your Own -- Really, Really Basic -- "Shampoo"

It's time to do something concrete this week, so why don't we experiment with something that costs a fair amount of money -- especially if you have teenaged girls in the house -- and doesn't necessarily have to.

Before we move on, I'll toss out the caveat that your teenaged daughters will gag at this idea, but you're a grown-up, so maybe you're willing to try it for yourself. It's so insanely simple that you'll be tempted to toss this book across the room and call me inappropriate names, but open your mind a little and give it a try.

- Baking soda.

- And vinegar.

Not together, by the way.

In an 8-ounce squeeze bottle, mix a cup of water with two tablespoons of baking soda and shake it together.

In another 8-ounce squeeze bottle, mix a scant cup of water with two tablespoons of vinegar and shake it together.

When you "shampoo," wet your hair, and squirt 1-3 ounces of the baking soda liquid over your scalp. Rub it in -- I count a hundred rubs, across my scalp -- let it sit for a minute, then rinse. The rubbing stimulates the scalp, and some people believe that this promotes hair growth. At any rate, massaging your scalp increases blood circulation to the area, and it's relaxing in a quiet sort of way.

Repeat this technique with the vinegar mixture.

That's it. I do this every two days, letting my hair rest one day in between.

Initially, your hair may seem greasy and heavy -- this is because, when we use standard shampoos, they "strip" the natural oils off of our scalp. As the day goes by, our body says, "OMG -- all the oil has been stripped off the scalp. I'd better make some more!" and your hair feels and looks greasy before the day is out.

When you use the baking soda/vinegar process, however, the natural oil is not stripped from your scalp. The rubbing removes dirt and other particles, and your hair is just left feeling clean. It may take a few days -- even a week or two -- for your head and hair to get used to the new hair product (your body's going to spend a few days in the "OMG -- all the oil's been stripped from my scalp" stage from your previous shampoo use), but if you're patient, it's worth trying. This natural approach to cleaning your hair is definitely cheaper, and there's the added benefit that you can pronounce all three ingredients -- baking soda, vinegar, and water.

You can also adjust the proportions of baking soda and vinegar to the uniqueness of your hair -- if your hair is too dry, decrease the baking soda and increase the vinegar; if your hair is too greasy, increase the baking soda and decrease the vinegar.

I use this "shampoo," as does the Norwegian Artist and Son and Heir, but Tired of Being Youngest won't touch it. She won't drink goat milk, either, so go figure?

Pretty Packaging

Talking about shampoo, and personal care products, brings up the concept of packaging, colors, images, and scents -- because personal care products, especially for females, are all about what the product looks like on the outside.

Mango passion fruit shampoo. Cool green cucumber conditioner. Vanilla and cinnamon sugar hand lotion. Strawberries and cream facial wash.

It's funny how all this stuff we put on our skin and hair appeals to things we want to eat. Maybe that's why we fall for them so heavily -- most females are constantly on some diet or another, denying themselves sensual treats for the mouth, so we compensate by slathering it on our hair.

But when you think about it, the scents and the flavors and the colors are artificial -- there's no actual mango in that foot cream, and if there were, would you rub it on your heels? If you make a commitment to live more naturally -- cooking from scratch for yourself, seeking out organic or not so pesticide laden produce, experimenting with making your own soap -- you'll naturally (pun sort of intended) gravitate away from fake, chemically-produced-in-a-lab products that mimic the real thing, without actually having anything of the real thing about it.

Consider the last chapter, and the baking soda/vinegar shampoo concoction. No mangoes. No vanilla and cinnamon sugar. No pinks and purple and sparkles and stripes. No bright plastic containers with pictures of hibiscus flowers on it. Just baking soda and water in one container (buy a bright one! you can probably find something at the dollar store outlet) and vinegar and water in the other.

It's cheap, and it works. If you want fruit and flowers and spices, then take the money you saved on the shampoo and buy the real stuff, the fruit you eat, the flowers you put on the table, the spices you cook with.

The next time you're in the store, pick up the brightest, happiest, smelliest bottle of shampoo; flip it over; and read through the ingredients. Most of them you won't be able to pronounce, and if you can't say them, much less know what they are, you might think twice about dumping them all over you head.

Now, pick up a cheap bottle of shampoo, flip it over, look at the ingredients, and compare them to the ones in the expensive bottle. Many of them, barring the flavors and scents and colors, may very well be the same, which means that whether you spend $10 or $1, you're paying for pretty much the identical product.

Walk an aisle or two down and pick up a bottle of liquid hand soap; compare the ingredients in this to some of those in the shampoo. I did this once, and was intrigued to find many similarities. No, they're not all the same, and with all those chemicals there are variations on the theme, but there's enough of a likeness to make me wonder how we can fill an entire aisle with bottle after bottle after bottle of different brands of the same product.

Go back to your expensive, bright, happy, beautiful, desirable bottle of shampoo and ask yourself these questions:

1) If this product were in a clear plastic container, would I be tempted to buy it?

2) If I had never seen an ad for this product, would I be tempted to buy it?

3) If I buy this particular brand of shampoo, will I really look like Heidi Klum?

Beware of pretty packaging, whether it's in the personal care, cereal, or underwear aisle. The more flowers and bright colors and cool green cucumbers you see (or, if you're a man, ripped abs and people flying through the air on snowboards, and yes, I know that I'm being outrageously sexist but don't let this get in the way of the message), the more you want to pause and look at the actual product itself, bereft of packaging.

- What is it that you're buying?

- Is it truly worth what's being charged?

- Is there an alternative that costs less?

- Is there an alternative that you can create or make yourself?

Constantly ask yourself questions, analyze why you are attracted to a certain product, figure out how you are being drawn into this purchase -- because that is what the people who made these products have spent a lot of time doing.

119

Is their marketing strategy working?

If you're like me, you don't want to answer "yes," to this question, so step back for a minute (remembering that you're in a store aisle and you don't want to back up into anybody) and ask yourself,

"If this were in a glass jar, and if the product inside were clear or uncolored, would I be compelled to purchase it?"

"Is there anything significantly superior about this product that differentiates it from a cheaper brand?"

"Am I being attracted by the scent (which is chemically induced, by the way), the pictures on the bottle, the text on the package, or memories of commercials I have endured that feature this product?"

Before we close this chapter, let me tell you a story:

Years ago I read a children's tale, the kind in an elementary school reader, that described a little girl who needed a new pair of shoes so that she could go on a school field trip to the zoo. Her other pair, we inferred, were too distressed for her to be seen out in public wearing them.

"Here is the money for the shoes," her father said, and handed her cash (remember, this is a tale from my childhood, which precedes, by many years, debit cards).

"Father," the little girl said. "I saw some beautiful colored jars that I want so badly to decorate the top of my dresser. May I have those as well?"

(Remember, again, that this is an elementary school reader, not known for gripping dialogue or engaging prose.)

"There's not enough money to buy both," he replied. "If you buy the jars, you can't buy the shoes, and if you don't buy the shoes, you can't go on the field trip."

Well, obviously the child bought the jars -- three of them, a gorgeous violet, and filled with liquid. The first thing she did upon returning home was to open the lid of the first jar and pour out the liquid.

"I'll put rocks or trinkets inside," she thought. "They'll look so pretty with the violet."

Well, guess what. Once the girl dumped out the liquid -- which was violet, by the way -- she was left with an empty, clear jar, because the color that she had admired so much came from the liquid inside.

So not only is she stuck with a bad purchase, made to look better only because of the way it was packaged, she also couldn't go on the school field trip, because she didn't have a new pair of shoes.

Let the buyer beware.

Cheap Entertainment

We are fortunate in this country that we do not have to labor, from dawn to dusk and beyond, to grow the food that winds up on our table. Leisure time is a reality for many of us, and while it is a blessing indeed, if we don't watch ourselves, it can be a financial drain as well.

Take movies, for example. We know people who regularly attend -- and by regularly I mean twice a month or more -- and each time they purchase popcorn, pop (ah, but if they read the chapter in this book on that, they would no more do so!), and other treats. It's important to them to have seen the latest movie and to be up on the most recent cinematic events.

And there we go again -- when what other people think about you and your lifestyle matters, you make decisions that aren't the best for you, financially. Even if you love movies, you can wait. Six months from now, when it's rentable on DVD, it will still be as good, or bad, as it was on the big screen.

And while it's fun to see things on the big screen, not every movie demands the experience.

Bowling, ice skating, gym memberships, monthly product clubs, dinners out, getaways to a hotel -- there are endless ways to spend money in our leisure time, and while it's not a mortal sin to indulge in fun things that cost money, it's not such a bad idea to limit the splurging and choose wisely and well.

And then, we can replace some of those fun things that cost money with fun things that don't. Here are a few ideas:

- Visit your library and take full advantage of its music and media rental. Check out books of all sorts, and get that little rush of coming home with a pile of reading material. I know, this is generally the first item on any list about doing free things, but that's probably for a reason. The public library is a vastly underused and underrated resource that is open to just about all of us.

- If you have a digital reader, explore some of the public domain books from yesteryear. Many of these are free; some are $0.99, and while yes, that old stuff sounds different from what's written today, it's not such a bad idea to train your brain to read it. Makes you more patient.

- Prepare a family or friend dinner together and make it special. Spend time around the table talking, afterwards; every week, our Sunday mornings stretch close to noon as we pour yet another cup of tea and launch into another subject of conversation.

- Take a walk with one another. The Norwegian Artist and I have been taking daily walks for more than 30 years, and I can assure you, one good way to get on really good, comfortable speaking terms with another person is to walk with them for an hour a day.

- Got someone you love in another town? Write them a letter. E-mails, texts, and phone calls are the communication methods of the 21st century, but nothing beats a letter, hands down. Every Sunday, I sit down -- on the sunny porch if it's warm enough, on the living room sofa if it's not -- and hand write a letter to whatever children of mine who aren't within face-to-face visiting distance. I consider it one of the most important things I do all week.

- While you're at it, create a card for that person. You don't need material beyond stiff paper, scissors, glue, and stuff to cut up and glue. When a relative was undergoing cancer treatment, we undertook to create a card for him from one of us, every day of the week. As there were six of us at the time, we managed to get the cards for the week prepared in one afternoon. It was a comfortable, warm time of togetherness, and we remember it with smiles to this day (and the relative remembers, and has kept, the cards).

- Sit with a kitty.

- Invite friends over for a potluck, and just talk together. Our potlucks are generally so ad hoc that the preparation conversation goes like this: (Them) "What do you want us to bring?" (Us) "Whatever you've got. We'll do soup and bread." It really doesn't matter if all you end up with is soup and bread; it's not as if we don't get enough to eat in this country, but we frequently don't get enough time with one another.

- Learn to knit. Of course, that's my activity, and it's a good one because, although it costs money to buy yarn, knitting a project generally takes so long that you amortize that expense over days, weeks, or months. Plus, you wind up with something you can wear.

- Okay, so you don't want to learn to knit. But learn to do something that involves creating -- sewing, knitting, painting, writing, gardening, building birdhouses. Yes, it costs money to purchase supplies, but as with knitting, the amount of time it takes to complete the project amortizes the investment.

- Don't feel guilty about Netflix. I was reading through some "money-saving" guides recently, and one of the repeated mantras was "Get rid of Netflix. Don't go to the Red Box. Stop spending money on renting movies." You know, renting movies -- as long as you limit yourself -- or belonging to a monthly club for $10 or so, is really cheap entertainment, and two hours of streaming one movie into your living room amortizes out to $5 an hour. If you watch four two-hour movies a month, you're talking $1.25 an hour. That's really cheap entertainment, and unless you're in absolute sacrificial mode, you can probably afford this. Just be aware of what a great deal it is, and don't take it for granted. Make your movie nights special -- pop your own popcorn, pour a glass of milk (you've dropped pop, remember?) and think to yourself, "I'm sitting in my living room, watching an amazing movie that cost $125 million to make, and it's amortizing out to less than $1.25 an hour. Am I smart, or what?"

You'll notice that a lot of these suggestions have less to do with *doing* something as they do with *being* with others, even if the other person you're with is a dead guy who wrote a book 150 years ago.

If you hate each and every one of my suggestions, at least enter into the spirit of the thing and kick around some ideas of your own. What can you do, in a free afternoon, that doesn't involve purchasing an admission ticket?

Your Very, Very Private Exercise Club

While we're discussing saving money on entertainment, let's talk about your exercise plan.

I'm sure you have one -- don't we all, from January 1 through January 23?

In our little town, there is a gym on Main Street that consists of a series of machines upon which you run, jog, or flail about in some manner or another, and it fascinates me that, because of the large windows, anyone driving by can see in. Especially at night.

Maybe I'm just an extra, extra private person, but when I'm sweaty, disheveled, breathing hard and dressed in sweat pants, I really don't want others watching.

But that isn't the only reason I don't belong to this gym. Membership requires an up-front down payment and a monthly financial commitment of at least 6 months, and while I understand the theory behind this -- if you've made a financial commitment you're more likely to stick to your exercise plan -- I don't spend my money this way.

The foundation of my exercise plan has stayed the same for more than 30 years -- I walk 3-5 miles each day, generally with the Norwegian Artist, and we use that time to talk, to dream, to explore ideas, to (on a limited basis) discuss politics, to just . . . talk, really.

The added benefit of this particular exercise plan is that our marriage is in great shape, since it's very difficult to walk closely beside someone for 45 minutes to an hour each day and not communicate. On the few occasions when we've been just plain mad at one another, we either hash it out or cut the walk short. The dog prefers it when we do the former.

Walking is great exercise and it's pretty much free. You can do it anywhere, and even if you have kids, you can keep up the program: as ours started arriving, we invested in a double-seated racing stroller and just kept moving. Because we cleverly arranged the spacing of 2-3 years between each child (not really on the clever part; but they are all well spaced), by the time a new one was ready to go in, an older one was gently booted out and taught how to ride a bicycle.

When we want to add to our individual exercise plans, the Norwegian Artist and I each do it our unique way: I'll invest in an exercise DVD and closet myself upstairs in the studio with it, with strict instructions for no one to be in the same building (although when Tired of Being Youngest was younger, we lifted weights together); the Norwegian chops wood, or builds greenhouses, or digs garden plots, something I define as extra work and he considers healthy outdoor living.

As a society, we have bought, literally, into the notion that exercise is a separate activity, one that ideally needs to be pursued in a gym, or with a classroom group, or requiring special equipment or membership fees. Exercise, at its base, is no more than getting off our butts and moving those butts around, along with our arms and abs and lower back and shoulders -- you don't have to know what pectoral muscles are to use them.

If you're like the Norwegian Artist, and you want to get something done while you're exercising, then get stuff done. If you're tired and sore afterwards, you can bet that you exercised some set of muscles, somewhere.

If you're like me, and you feel like there's enough work going on already and you look at exercise as "me" time, then do your thing -- there are plenty of great resources in book, DVD, or online (often free!) form to instruct you in what it is that you want to do, providing that what you want to do isn't climb Mount Everest.

But don't forget about walking. It's one of those all-purpose activities that requires no equipment (yes, there are arguments about "proper" shoes, but there are just as many arguments about going barefoot, the ultimate in free), prep-time, classroom instruction, or licensing -- you open the door, step out to the sidewalk, hallway, or lawn, and get started.

Throughout the years I have encouraged people, especially couples, to take advantage of this free, healthy relationship improving opportunity, but while I've seen groups of women power walk together, I have never met another couple who spends their time this way.

Sometime this week, if you don't walk already, take a walk. Being outside with the sky so far overhead, you find yourself focusing less on the problems that weigh on your mind, and those very problems seem smaller, farther away, more manageable. They won't be gone once the walk is done, but maybe they will seem a tiny bit less overwhelming, and the good feelings engendered by fresh air and exercise last longer than the walk itself.

Start a Garden

Don't you just love generalized, sweeping statements that encapsulate all sorts of work and planning and complication within one simple sentence like, "Pay off your house," "Get out of debt," or "Start a garden"?

If you've stuck with me this long, you know I don't expect you to make eight years worth of changes in one week, and I certainly don't want to pressure you into thinking that this is possible.

But starting a garden doesn't have to be a massive undertaking, and it's something you can do even if you're in an apartment -- providing, of course, that you have a window somewhere that allows in light. And if you've got a yard, this doesn't mean that you have to go dig the whole thing up and plant tomatoes and feed your entire family on what you grow alone.

Just plant something -- one plant is fine, two if you feel adventurous, a row of peas if you're really reckless, but Just. Plant. Something.

My second daughter, College Girl, lives in an apartment in Arizona, and on the phone the other day she mentioned how much she enjoys fresh herbs in her food, but they're so expensive to buy that she never uses as many of them as she'd like.

"You live in hot, warm climate that isn't in danger of blizzards," I replied. "Why don't you buy a window box --

the kind you'd put flowers in -- stick it on your balcony, and grow the herbs yourself?"

"You can grow your own herbs?" she replied. (Honestly, sometimes you wonder how they managed to live with you for years and years and years and never notice anything you're doing.)

Basil, oregano, chives, sage, rosemary -- you can find these plants already started in little pots and just transplant them to a larger one (rosemary, especially, is one you want to buy as a plant; it takes forever to germinate). Cilantro, which isn't excited about being transplanted, is easily started from seed. Curb your excitement about clipping your seedlings for dinner until they're big enough to handle it -- six to nine inches high or so -- but if you're like me, you snip bits and pieces even when they're small because you can't resist.

Herbs are great plants to start with because they generally don't require rich, well-worked soil -- think of where many of the Mediterranean based herbs grow; that's right, the Mediterranean, which is known for being dry and rocky. Most of them grow fast; and they're pretty resilient about being awkwardly treated by a novice gardener.

A tomato plant is a fun project as well -- beginning in April or so you can find them in the lawn and garden section of the box stores, and they do well in the ground or in a pot. Someday, if you really get into the whole gardening thing, you can start tomatoes and peppers and celery and pumpkins from seed, but until then, if then ever happens, just buy an already existent plant, and limit yourself to a small enough project that you can handle it.

Make sure the plant isn't droopy and sad looking (this can happen in the big retailers with the seasonal garden centers), and be aware that if the plant looks really big for the size of pot that it's in, it may be root bound -- that is, the little root hairs have wound themselves around and around the dirt in the pot because they haven't had anywhere to go. Bigger isn't necessarily better -- something that looks like it has been consistently well watered and stands up perky and straight, will eventually grow once you replant it.

By the way, you might notice that I keep reiterating the concept of one plant. Or two. Just because your neighbor is out there with the backhoe and the shifting cow manure pile and the gigantic garden that absorbs hours and hours of his time does not mean that you have to plunge into this project to the same level that he does.

Do what works for you, keep it fun, and see if you want to continue at the same rate or gently expand.

Be aware that once you start to research the concept of gardening, you will run into the whole homesteading and self-sufficiency camp -- and while there's nothing wrong with this concept (it's a positive thing to want to do as much for ourselves as we can), it is not the right lifestyle for everybody. And it doesn't have to be all or nothing.

Take us, for instance. For years, we grew a very small garden, even though we have 7 acres to grow one on, simply because we didn't have the time to devote to working the ground, planting, watering, weeding, replanting, more weeding, harvesting, and more weeding. Gardens can be a lot of work, which is also why they're a great source of exercise, and while they can be remarkably easy to start, they are not so easy to maintain and keep up.

Lately, we have expanded the garden, because our schedule enables us to do so, but there's still a lot of work.

Our garden tends to be a relaxed thing, in that it's not something you would find at Mr. Darcy's Pemberley of Jane Austen's *Pride and Prejudice*. We know one family that stakes out their garden with measuring tape and a ruler, so that it's completely straight, and they eliminate each and every weed before it even knows that it exists.

Us? We maintain reasonably straight rows, and we keep the weeds down especially when the plants are small so that they don't have to compete, but once the garden plants grow more vigorous and tall, we obsess less about the weeds. The ultimate purpose of our garden is to grow food, not impress others by how weed-free everything is.

And by the way, we don't spray or use artificial chemicals -- herbicides, pesticides, or fertilizers -- on our food, because we don't want to ingest that stuff. Doesn't matter to me if people say it's safe -- many of these people saying this are the ones making money off of selling it. So this means that, while we have more weeds than some of the people around us, we also have produce that requires no more than a swish of water to clean off the dirt.

Do you want something fast and easy that you can have on your table in a few short weeks? Plant lettuce and radishes; if the weather's warm enough you'll be harvesting something within 4-6 weeks. Butter crunch lettuce is succulent and tasty, and you can clip the leaves from the plant without having to wait to harvest the entire head.

Pumpkins, which take the whole summer to grow and are harvested in the fall, almost thrive on neglect. We have tossed out seeds in an unused space and forgotten about them, except for watering, and come October we've filled a wheelbarrow full of a product that is far more useful than just making jack o'lanterns out of.

If you've never gardened before, let me repeat myself: start small, and just focus on one or two plants. Baby the things. Figure out how they work. Enjoy the product of your first harvest, and don't worry that it doesn't cut your grocery store bill in half. Just experience the experience of growing a plant that produces something that you can eat, and enjoy the feeling of success that this engenders.

Start small. Start easy. Keep it fun, and customize it to what works for you.

Do I Have to Can Vegetables and Jam?

Let's be honest with ourselves.

Generally, when we ask a question that starts out with, "Do I have to . . .?" we sincerely hope that the answer is, "no."

Which means, that if you asked the question at the head of this chapter, you probably don't want to spend hours in July over a steaming stove making raspberry jam, or pressure canning green beans, or making pickles.

Some people really, really enjoy doing this, and they get great pleasure out of seeing the pint and quart glass jars of their creations, many of which preserve the bounty of their garden, or represent seasonally cheap prices on locally grown produce.

Other people -- I come immediately to mind -- hate doing this, and shudder at the sight of a 45-pound box of rapidly ripening peaches. Not only that, but I don't like the taste of canned peaches.

I do, however, love fresh jam, made with raspberries or strawberries or blackberries from our property, and as long as I don't have to produce 120 quarts of the product, I'm fine with making jam.

As with the gardening that we talked about in the chapter before this, too often we approach our projects with an all or nothing attitude:

1) We don't can or preserve at all. Anything.

135

2) We can everything. Enough to feed our family and several others.

I don't know if we need a 1B, or if we could make option number 2 into number 3, so that we can have a third, realistic option in between the two extremes:

We can or preserve as much or as little as we like, and we enjoy the process as a means of creating a fine food product out of quality ingredients.

I like making jam, within reason, and last year I made 20 quarts or so along with my daughter, Eldest Supreme. Raspberry, blackberry, peach -- there was enough to get us through the winter, and we enjoyed the fruits of our labor on pancakes, bread, and atop Danish pastries (which we made; Tired of Being Youngest, our, um, youngest, is a culinary student, and our favorite and most fattening academic quarter was Bake Shop).

If you have never canned or preserved before, making jam is a good place to start -- you'll need proper canning jars (not mayonnaise jars or old commercial jam jars, whatever anyone tells you) which you can buy used; lids and rims, which you can find in the baking section of your grocery store; a canning pot, which runs under $20 in a box store; some fruit; pectin (which thickens the jam); and a recipe (the pectin generally has an insert with nominal directions).

Make one batch, not six, over the entire day. You and I are not my grandmother, who had 11 children to feed through the winter, and she canned and preserved everything -- and you know something else about her? She was tired. All the time.

Too often there is this pressure that we need to live as they did in the 19th century, catching rabbits for stew and frying up cornbread over the old campfire spider, after a full day at the office. Most of us have the luxury of not starving if we don't trap that evening's dinner, and we frequently get so overwhelmed by what we're told we must do if we embark on a project, like canning, that we stop before we get started.

So just do one batch, and enjoy the process.

If your jam doesn't turn out and it's syrupy as opposed to spreadable, then just call it syrup instead of jam and use it as such.

Vegetables -- like green beans, corn, carrots, asparagus -- are low in acidity, and they cannot be safely canned unless you use a pressure canner, something that costs and involves more. I personally don't like the concept that one can acquire very serious, life threatening conditions from improperly canned vegetables, and I've never wanted to go through the necessary steps to ensure that I can safely produce a product that I have never found tasty or palatable in the first place.

As you'll see in the next chapter, Eat in Season, you can forego eating July's green beans in January by saving aside pumpkins from your garden and using those instead (not in the cute mushroom soup casserole with the dried crispy onions atop), or buy and use potatoes/carrots/onions and other winter friendly, cheap in-season vegetables and focus your January meals on that.

If you're awash in green beans and you really want to preserve the harvest, consider drying, with a dehydrator, the excess, or freezing them (and by the way, you don't just stick them in a baggy and toss them in a freezer; most vegetables that are to be frozen are blanched, or lightly cooked in water, first, then cooled, then packaged for freezing; this preserves the texture and taste).

If you don't want so many green beans and don't want to worry about saving them for the future, then consider doing two things: 1) don't plant so many next year and 2) give the excess away. Oh, and there's always option #3, the one that my Son and Heir constantly points out to me:

"Use them, Mom."

It drives him nuts, in July when raspberries are bursting out everywhere, that I buy bananas.

"Don't buy any fruit, Mom. Focus on raspberries."

So focus on beans, if you have them, and get creative about using them. You and your family are not going to collapse if you eat green beans every single night for four straight weeks, and if you get serious about looking for recipes, you don't have to have them as an ubiquitous side dish.

And then if you still have too many beans, there's still options 2 and 1, and option 4, if you have chickens -- feed them to the chickens. Oh, and option 5 -- put them in the compost pile.

Eat in Season

A lot is written these days about eating locally, both as a means of saving money and saving the planet, and it's not such a bad idea. If you do not have time or desire, however, to frequent Farmer's Markets and seasonal fruit stands, you can still benefit by the concept of eating local by eating seasonally.

Fresh strawberries do not grow naturally in the Pacific Northwest in January. If you are insistent upon having them, they will come from far away and they will cost a lot. Better to wait until June, when they do grow in the Pacific Northwest, they will cost less, and they will most likely be locally grown. In January, oranges are cheap, and while these do not grow in the Pacific Northwest, whether it's June or January, they are seasonally available. So in our household, in January, we eat oranges. (Bananas, incidentally, are definitely not local, but for some reason or another, they're always around and they're always relatively cheap; when everything else is expensive, we eat bananas.)

Salad greens are another item that we think we need to have all the time. I mean, who's going to argue about a salad? Aren't we supposed to get our vegetables?

Well, variety's a great thing, and in January, when lettuce isn't a major product grown in the northern part of the United States, cabbage is cheap, and you can make a salad out of finely shredded cabbage and carrots. Or gently stir fry it with sliced onions and the carrots -- wintertime is a great time to work with root vegetables -- like potatoes, sweet potatoes, carrots, and parsnips -- and winter brassicas: broccoli, cabbage, and cauliflower. There's plenty of time for salads in the summer.

Eating seasonally -- choosing foods that are inexpensive because they're widely available at a particular time -- is not only cheaper, it provides variety, and enables us to graze different foods for different vitamins, minerals, and health benefits. If you eat the same salad all year, you'll get the same food nutrients, but if you nosh on pumpkin in November, broccoli in February, spinach in April, and zucchini in July, you'll get all sorts of additional nutritional benefits, not to mention, visual and culinary interest from eating different foods.

Don't be boring in your eating habits. This week, as you're shopping for groceries, take a look at what is on sale and inexpensive, and determine that you will buy one of these items and make something out of it. The more versatile you are in your eating habits, the more you can save money, because you are not stuck buying the same things you always buy, regardless of the price.

Eat Together

Because we homeschooled our children, we avoided the trap many families find themselves in -- the 5 p.m. rush after work to the gym to watch a son or daughter play (or frequently, sit on the bench and watch other teammates play) basketball, soccer, volleyball, football, baseball -- public schools do really well at running sports programs.

On the few occasions I found myself in a fluorescently lighted high school gym when I would usually have been at home, sitting around the table with my family, eating dinner, I was definitely not in a happy place. I like eating dinner with my family. A banana and a peanut butter sandwich, hastily shoved into a bag and washed down with a bottle of water, just isn't the same thing. And most of the people around me weren't contenting themselves with something they brought from home.

Whether you work outside of your home, inside your home, or a combination of both, by the time 5 p.m. rolls by, you're tired and ready to rest (unless, of course, you work a swing shift, which means that you need to customize your life to find this time to rest), but all too many people find themselves shifting from the work-day to sports-night, and after the game, a "brief" meeting for the church or the non-profit-agency or school or whatever establishment bites off and chews more of their time that they really don't have.

Enter the family dinner hour. And if you're single, you're still a family, and you deserve this time devoted to the preparation of your meal, the getting away from outside obligations, the enjoyment of good food. It's too easy to get

141

into the habit of eating over the sink -- because it's just you -- and to feel that the company of one isn't worth anything. Are you kidding? You're an amazing person, and you NEED this time to focus on your meal. Regardless of the size of your household, make the family dinner hour a priority.

Years ago, there were newspaper ads and TV commercials and other media forums encouraging people to sit down and eat together; some of these communications were put out by non-profit organizations, others by manufacturers that made frozen dinners, but the overall message is a good one:

Families thrive on time spent together, and one of the easiest ways to spend this time together is to eat with one another. The whole process of preparing the meal, setting the table, consuming food, exchanging the day's stories, and cleaning up isn't just something to get through and get over with -- it is a valuable means of spending time all on its own. Eating dinner together is education, entertainment, group dynamics, community interaction, all those impressive terms and sociological concepts rolled collectively into a regular one-hour event that we can choose to participate in and enjoy every night.

Those are the unseen benefits. The tangible benefits -- money saved -- are quickly realized as multiple people share one meal as opposed to purchasing separate -- and individually more expensive -- meals from white bags, or on paper plates, or in foam cups. Night after night after night of that -- even if only one or two people are doing it -- adds up.

When you set out to live differently, initially because you want to save money, you gradually start to find that normal, day to day activity -- like eating dinner together -- becomes increasingly important, and activities that you once thought of as chores or work -- chopping vegetables, making coffee, putting away dishes -- are opportunities to think, meditate, converse with one another, and interact.

When we first moved out onto our 7-acre farmette, a relative visited and admired the view and ambience.

"But look at all the work you've got on your hands," he told Steve. "All those trees to plant and take care of, or grass to cut down, or animals to take care of. When do you have time to do fun things?"

"These are fun things," Steve replied. "Yes, it's work, but it's outside, and I'm getting exercise, and I feel proud of what I accomplish each day. I could spend money at a gym and get exercise, or I could dig in the garden -- and I have more fun in the garden. It's just adjusting the way you look at things."

That's what a saving-money lifestyle is -- adjusting the way you look at things, and finding pleasure and fulfillment in the small, ordinary chores that make up each of our days. Eating dinner, together, is one of those small, activities that has the potential to be a big, life-enhancing experience.

Unless we are subsistence farmers, which most of us in industrial nations are not, it's easy for us to forget that food is not something to be taken for granted. Many people, in many parts of the world, do not get enough of it, and those of us who do would be wise to approach our daily eating experience with gratitude, appreciation, and time.

Spend Your Time as Wisely as Your Money

In the last chapter I mentioned organized sports, and how much time (and money) they can wrest from individuals and families, and yet we continue to pursue them because 1) our children are taught to expect us to and 2) society expects us to.

Cheerfully attending each and every one of each and every child's sports and academic and educationally social events is an expectation that many of us don't question, because if we do, we are accused of being unsupportive, insensitive, and not interested in our children's lives.

Oh, please.

That we are tired ourselves, or don't particularly like football, or are over stimulated by the noise and the lights and the activity, isn't something that we are allowed to explore, but we would be kind to ourselves if we did.

Another kindness would be to question all extraneous activity in which we find ourselves -- either through work, school, church, volunteer groups, friends, clubs -- they add up fast. There are many, many establishments out there holding meetings, events, fundraisers, and activities -- and they expect us to be in attendance.

This is not to say that these establishments aren't valuable, or what they are having meetings about isn't meaningful (although I really, really question the value of most meetings), but just because something is good doesn't mean that we have to be a part of it.

Think of a potluck -- all those casseroles and stews and breads and desserts and drinks and chips and green beans mixed with soup and topped by those crunchy fried onions in a can -- no matter how good the food is, you can't eat all of it, and at some point, you make choices to skip two of the three scalloped potato dishes, because otherwise you won't have room for the lasagna.

So it is with life -- if you fill your evenings, weekends, and free time with meaningful meetings set up by worthwhile establishments, you don't have time to play cribbage with your teenager, or read a book to your toddler, or take a long hot bath, or pull weeds in the garden, or knit your first pair of socks. There simply aren't enough hours.

Unfortunately, we often choose to give our time -- which is a precious commodity indeed -- to the people who demand it the most strongly and loudly, and while we can't tell the boss that we're not in the mood to work a full day but we'd still like the paycheck, we can say no to a number of insistent, yet voluntary, obligations.

It's not easy -- nobody likes to hear the word, "No," but every time we say "yes" to someone's request for our time, we are potentially saying "no" to our own needs. Does this sound selfish? It's not -- disabuse yourself of the notion that you cannot reserve time for yourself without being perceived as selfish. Certain types of people catch on to this uncertainty, and they press hard on you with pernicious perspicacity, manipulating you into doing what's best for them, but not necessarily for you. It's not selfish to make decisions that are in your own -- or your family's -- best interest.

How do you know? Try this:

When it's time to head to the meeting, if you say -- or think -- something along the lines of,

"I hate going to these things on Tuesday nights. I can't wait until it's over," hold onto that thought.

After the meeting, if you have amended your thinking to something like this,

"I never want to go to these things, but I'm always so happy when I do," then don't give it up just yet.

But if you think, "I am so glad that thing is over until next week. I HATE these meetings," then ask yourself, "Why do I go to them anyway? And is there any way that I can stop?"

If you're wondering what this has to do with saving money, consider the savings in gas as you drive every place, as well as sundry dues and fees and purchases associated with the group holding the meetings -- those are tangible expenses. Think, also, of the quick meal you grab because you don't have time for dinner -- with the family -- beforehand, or the magazine you purchase as a treat to yourself for giving up your time. Maybe you'll pick up smoking again. Or grab a can of pop. The little expenses may be difficult to identify but they are there -- because when you are overworked, overstressed, and under relaxed, you tend to spend money on frivolous items.

Learn to say no.

"Overwhelmed" Is Not the New Normal

You're making a lot of changes these days, and anytime you're out to make changes, it's easy to feel overwhelmed. I was reminded of this recently after wandering through various food, family, and homeschooling Facebook and blog sites. The word "overwhelmed," was showing up entirely too much. Like this:

"I am homeschooling a five-year-old and I have a toddler and a new baby. The curriculum takes 4 hours a day, and I feel overwhelmed."

"I'm trying to feed my family more healthfully, after years of eating take-out, and I feel overwhelmed by how much time it takes and how much it costs."

"I just went back to work full time, and I've been feeling overwhelmed by the laundry, food preparation, and shopping."

Maybe it's just distance or age (which I hope is as much associated with wisdom as it is crow's feet), but I looked at the first woman and thought,

"The child is 5. Are you trying to do too much?"

And the second, "Eating healthfully is a lifestyle, and you don't adopt it overnight."

And the third, "Nobody else in the house knows how to cook?"

To all three readers I wanted to say, "Slow down. Breathe. You're pushing yourself too hard -- and probably trying to live by somebody else's standards."

The word "overwhelmed," is a symptom of a problem. I know that sounds obvious, but what most people don't realize is that, when you're overwhelmed, the problem isn't you. The goals that you are setting for yourself -- and how you are telling yourself that you will reach them -- are the problem. Not you -- it's not that you're inept or lazy or unintelligent or not working hard enough -- it's that you're asking yourself to do more than you are able to do right now.

Too often, when we try new things -- like homeschooling or healthy eating or radically changing about how we think about money -- we rely upon the expertise of others, but some of these others have been doing for years what we're just starting, and they've got their own way of doing it.

And no matter how long we wind up doing what we're just starting, we may never do it another person's way. For instance, when my oldest was five (and the second was 2, and I was pregnant with the third), we homeschooled by sitting on the couch and reading books. It was fun; the two-year-old wasn't ostracized; my lower back got a rest; we all learned various facts about the white rhinoceros and the Indian elephant; and most importantly, I wasn't overwhelmed to the point that I wanted to give the whole thing up. I found something that worked for me, and I did it. Someone else will accomplish the same task a different way.

Eating more healthfully is a continuous process for our family that began 20 years ago, and every day we do something a little different, to the point that the bean soup with Gjetost cheese we had for lunch today would have been an unimaginable aberration 20 years ago. At the same point, two weeks ago I bought and enjoyed a cream-filled doughnut. I have forgiven myself; I hope that others can.

Wherever you are in your goals and life changes, be there, and not in the middle of somebody else's experience. Recognize that you learn a little bit more each day, and you add one day's experience to the next, so that when enough time goes by, you will have made, and internalized, some significant changes. If you meet someone new to the whole thing, be kind, and share your experiences gently, not as if they are paradigms for the rest of the world to follow.

The only hard and fast rule about doing new things in your life and doing them well is this:

When you feel overwhelmed, something's wrong, and it's time to step back and figure out just what it is. Overwhelmed is not the new normal.

Celebrate

Fifteen years ago, when we started building our house, we kept telling ourselves, "We are SO going to celebrate once we finish this house!"

We were doing the actually building ourselves, and paying for the project as we went, so while, 15 years later, we completely own our house and do not have, and never did have, a mortgage, we also do not have a precisely completed house. There's the matter of a finished floor, window trim, and rocks on the chimney.

But that hasn't stopped us from celebrating.

While we haven't yet had the big bash for the finished house, we celebrate little things, all the time -- birthdays, anniversaries, the planting of the spring garden, the first tomato, the weekly survival to Friday -- celebrating doesn't have to be big, expensive, lavish, or loud, but it is nice when it's frequent.

Awhile ago, when we were newlyweds, an older couple with whom we were close invited us to dinner, in celebration of their anniversary. While we loved the thought of being with them and eating out, we were reluctant to crash their anniversary.

"It's your day," we said. "We don't want to get in the way."

"You are our dear friends, and a part of who and what we are," they replied. "What better way to celebrate our anniversary than with people whom we love?"

Good point.

This couple's open, embracing attitude toward life and love affected the way we thought about celebrations, and our own anniversary fetes include all of the progeny we can get our hands on. In earlier years, I made a special dinner -- shrimp, pasta primavera, asparagus, cheesecake, homemade bread -- the amount of money it took to feed six of us as much as we wanted would have paid for one meal at a fine restaurant.

Later, as the progeny grew up and older and into really good cooks, they divided the chores and created the dinner themselves. One of our favorite activities, still, is to calculate the cost of the dinner, per person, in restaurant prices and multiply by the number of people eating. I can assure you that we spend much, much less than that.

When I don't know how to make something, I ask; the meat man at the local grocery spent 20 minutes with me instructing how to butterfly shrimp; another time, he gave me an intense lesson on grilling steaks to perfection. Maybe he's unique, but I've found that many people at the grocery store, if you catch them when they're not insanely busy, are pleased and flattered to share with you the benefits of their experience and expertise. It never hurts to ask.

If you spend your entire life waiting for projects to be officially done before you celebrate them -- like our house -- you'll never celebrate; maybe that's why birthdays happen once a year -- you don't have to be complete or perfect to age, and since you're going to do it anyway, you may as well be thankful for the extra year, and grateful for the people around you who went through life with you that year. Celebrating is nothing more than taking time from our obligations and focusing on our blessings.

- Did you drop pop out of your life this week? Celebrate!

- How about exercising? Don't worry that you haven't lost ten pounds yet -- did you take walks this week and make an effort to be active? Celebrate!

- Did you save money this week by bringing lunch to work instead of importing white paper-bagged products from places you drive through? Celebrate!

- Is it the end of the school quarter? Celebrate!

- How about the end of the week, and tomorrow you get to sleep in? Celebrate!

Make a special meal, brew a pot of tea and drink it sitting around the coffee table, splurge on a $7 bottle of wine (believe me, in our house, that's fine wine), pop some popcorn and watch a movie -- celebrating doesn't have to be complex, complicated, convoluted, or difficult. Celebrating is an attitude of publicly and privately expressing gratitude for whatever it is you are glad about, and because life itself is a journey, we don't wait until we get to our final destination to enjoy some of the benefits of the journey.

You are making changes, day by day and bit by bit, in how you look at money and spend it, and each one of these changes is worth recognizing, being grateful for, and celebrating. Success is not a one-time event at the end of the finish line; it is a daily event, and as we train ourselves to look for the positive changes and good things in our life, the more we focus on what we have, as opposed to lamenting about what we have not.

We do that a lot, don't we? We focus on what we don't have, and if we can't remember what we don't have, we remind ourselves by looking around at other people, and comparing. Coveting -- I mentioned it in the introduction -- is never a good idea, and the fruit it produces is always sour.

But celebrating -- taking time to think about what we have and to be joyful about it -- results in the opposite: sweet feelings of gratitude and contentment. Ultimately, isn't that what we're looking for? We have the mistaken notion that this is something that can be purchased -- a vacation, a new car, a big screen television -- and we envision the fun things that we will do once we have these products, and how these fun things will make us feel.

But we've already got a lot of fun things in our lives. Unless we take the time to recognize that they're there however, we won't get the full measure of joy that they can bring us.

So celebrate. Anything.

Create

Years ago I read a critique of the American society (there are a lot of those) that described one of our major problems being that we consume more than create. This describes us not only as a nation, but as individuals.

While we have little impact or voice in the hallowed halls of politics, we are each responsible for our own lives, and one by one, we can make a difference. We can start that difference by getting a hobby. In the long run, this enables us to save money on our household finances.

"So how do I save money by purchasing supplies and equipment for developing a hobby?" you ask.

Good question -- first of all, choose your hobby carefully, and enter it slowly, so that you spend more time doing whatever it is that you're creating, than you do money on supplies.

Here's an example: knitting.

Knitting is a hobby that can be entered with a minimum of financial overlay; you pretty much need a pair of knitting needles, some yarn, and a pattern. I know from experience that you can spend a LOT of money on yarn; I also know that the projects I made with the Bactrian Camel Hair yarn took weeks to complete -- a pair of socks, fingerless gloves, and a decorative element in a hat -- and all of those projects are still in use, years later. What I spent in yarn was well reaped during the actual knitting, not to mention the use of the finished projects.

I could have invested the same amount in a large pizza and two theater tickets -- sheer consuming -- and resulted with nothing to show for it.

So yes, knitting costs me money for supplies -- but it pays back in hours of entertainment, an increased level of skill, the sense of pride that you get from creating anything, and the resultant project. If stocks paid dividends at this level, we'd all look like brilliant investors.

Gardening, painting, writing, woodworking, sewing, cooking, keeping chickens -- these home-based, domestic crafts enable us to create for ourselves products that are generally produced for us -- vegetables, artwork, home decor, clothing, two layer frosted layer cakes. There is a feeling of empowerment and pride in wearing a pair of knitted socks that not only looks nicer than what you buy in dozens at the box store, but which will last much, much longer.

You realize that you are not dependent upon "others" for everything that you use, and that with a little work and ingenuity, you can create something that you want, need, and use. You also start to look at other purchases with a critical eye, and when you are faced with hydroponically grown, tasteless tomatoes in February, you tell yourself, "I grow far superior tomatoes than these. I can wait until August for the real thing." And because you know how to cook, you make something for dinner that night that doesn't require fresh tomatoes (most of the time, incidentally, you can replace a can of decent canned, chopped tomatoes for the water-grown stuff, and it's far, far cheaper).

With the money that you spend on your hobby, you are 1) learning a skill, 2) getting something tangible in return for the supplies invested, and 3) achieving the rush of pride and joy from creating, as opposed to consuming. Watching a movie, or any similar passive activity, does not pay out these same benefits.

If you use what you create (and I recommend this -- when you wear what you sew or eat what you bake, you are your own best critic, and you figure out what needs to be improved; if you give away everything you make, your recipients may be reluctant to inform you where you need to improve, and you'll never advance) you tend to use less, because it takes time to make more. Pajama pants come to mind -- consisting of pretty much four pieces and not requiring any tailoring or fitting, pajama pants are a fast, quick, cheap project for beginning sewers, and if the result isn't perfect, who cares? You're not wearing them to the office.

But you chose the fabric for them, you made them, you're proud of them, and you wear them again and again and again, getting the most out of the money you invested. You don't need five pairs, and if you really insist that you do, you can achieve them slowly, making them one by one.

Before we leave the concept of hobbies, here's one thing to keep in mind:

Making things yourself is not always cheaper than buying them, especially at the beginning of the hobby when you're not very good and you don't get the results you want. This is especially true of sewing -- fabric is expensive, and it's hard to compete with cheap, not necessarily well crafted, textile products flooding into the box stores. But if you persist, and get really good, you will eventually create a customized product that is far superior to anything you can purchase in these box stores, with the added benefit that, every time you wear it, you feel a surge of pride and well being.

Do not underestimate the value of that surge of pride you get when you create something for yourself. It's priceless.

Make Soup

Canned soup has always fascinated me, because it's really fairly expensive stuff. Making soup at home is so phenomenally easy, cheap, and relatively fast, that it's sad it's such a mystery to people. But it doesn't have to be a mystery to you.

If you've never made soup before, or even haven't cooked much of anything before, you will be happiest if you internalize this one very important, salient fact:

Home cooked food does not taste like manufactured food sold in grocery stores.

Our first tendency is to think, "Home cooked food can't be as good then, because it doesn't taste like manufactured food," when really, the opposite is true. Manufactured food tends to be saltier, sweeter, and more homogenized in flavor than home cooked food because the primary directive is not taste, but cost.

But because it is what most of us have grown up with and are accustomed to, we compare the home product with the grocery store product, and if the former doesn't taste like the latter, then the home cooked product is deemed to be inferior. Shouldn't it be the other way around?

Years ago, we had a little girl over to visit for lunch, and we were having homemade chocolate pudding for dessert. A visiting friend of mine was absolutely baffled that I was reluctant to give the child the pudding.

"I thought that you were being mean," she told me later. "You kept asking her if she was sure she wanted to try it, because it wasn't from a package, and when you did give it to her, you gave her a very small portion."

Ah, but I knew this child, and more importantly, I knew how she was accustomed to eating: lots of fast food, packaged products, manufactured processed "food." I also knew that she was extremely picky.

The child took one small bite and pushed the rest of the bowl away. Homemade pudding does not taste like the stuff out of the box. (Interestingly, all the stuff out of the boxes, store brand or name creation, pretty much tastes the same.)

"After she refused to eat the pudding, I understood your motives," my friend concluded. "It's a shame to see good food wasted."

The more you eat home cooked food, made as much from scratch as possible from good ingredients, the more your taste buds will adjust until, eventually, home created food will taste normal. But if you're not there yet, don't throw your soup out because it doesn't taste like something out of a can -- it won't, I assure you, but if you use good ingredients (and pretty much anything you use will be better than what the factory tosses in) you will get a different -- yet superior -- flavor to your food.

Soup can be as complex or as simple as you like, and while purists will insist that you simmer a chicken for its stock (after you have raised and butchered it, of course), you can make a tasty soup base out of water and bouillon, so don't let complexity stop you before you've started trying.

Remember, this is *your* journey, and if you find yourself being unduly affected -- did you read the chapter about being overwhelmed? -- by the comments of others' that you're not going about this the right way, then stop, get their voices out of your head, and then go look through your fridge for the ingredients you'll need for tonight's dinner -- Fast, easy, cheap chicken soup.

Fast, Easy, Cheap Chicken Soup

From start to finish, this soup takes about an hour, with very little active work on your part. And it's cheap; I burrowed through the refrigerator and threw in what I could find, which, given the contents of my refrigerator, is sometimes odd. Feel free to mix and match with what's hanging around in your crisper.

Ingredients:

- **Water**
- **1 onion**, chopped
- **6 mini Portobello mushrooms**, chopped (these add depth and complexity to the dish; if you don't like mushrooms, skip 'em; if you have white buttons, use 'em; one time I used a little can. Making soup is remarkably flexible.)
- **1/2 cup chopped Delicata squash** (bet you don't have this; I do; I'm Awash with Squash; Delicata breaks down as it cooks and thickens the broth, but you could use a cup of **chopped celery** and or **carrots** instead; I didn't use celery because I didn't have it. Just don't use anything too demanding, like broccoli, kale, or cabbage.)
- **1 Tablespoon Chicken broth paste** (I use Better Than Bouillon organic, which I buy at Costco)
- **Two boneless, skinless chicken thighs or breasts**

- **Two teaspoons curry powder** (this stuff is pretty common, and you should be able to find it somewhere, some brand, in your grocery store. This is the link to curry powder at Amazon.com. This ingredient is also optional, if you're one of those people who really, really hates any kind of spice, but the turmeric that is the major component of traditional curry powder is one of those good-for-you ingredients that adds a novel taste to the experience.)

Bring 1 quart water to boil. Yes, I know that this is breaking all the rules of haute cuisine. But this isn't haute cuisine; it's home cuisine, and while it may not be something you pay $12.95 per bowl for at a fine restaurant, it's significantly better than anything you'll get out of a can.

Add the onions, squash/celery/carrots, mushrooms, and chicken bouillon paste and bring back to a boil. Lower stove heat to medium to maintain a high simmer; stir down the contents if they start to overflow; leave pot uncovered; and let vegetables cook for 30 minutes.

After 20 minutes, check to make sure the vegetables are soft. If not, cook longer until they are.

Add one more quart water and two boneless, skinless chicken thighs or breasts; my chicken thighs came straight from the freezer. Leave the heat at medium; cover the pot with a lid but not tightly -- leave the lid slightly askew so that there is a slight crack showing you the pot contents underneath; cook for 20-30 minutes more.

At the end of 20 minutes, take out the chicken pieces and chop them. If they're still pink, and mine were because I started with a frozen product, toss the chopped pieces back in for another five minutes. Otherwise, just toss the chopped pieces back in.

Add the curry powder if you're using it and salt to taste.

That's it. One hour, most of it spent watching water simmer, or better yet, knitting a sock.

Bon Appetit, and Good Health to you and yours.

Saving Money in the Grocery Store -- One Weird, Workable Idea

Years ago, with four children in tow, I spent one day a week doing the grocery shopping.

The night before I scoured the ads, marking this place for brown sugar and butter, that one for grapes and toilet paper, still another for vanilla extract. By the end of the day, we had hit pretty much every grocery store in the mid-sized town where we lived; the car was packed; the kids were tired; and nobody felt particularly good because lunch consisted of stuff off the cheap menu at the local Fast Fried Food Emporium.

Did I save money?

Well, I felt like I did, but I always knew that there was a lot more in the trunk than what was on my list (did I mention the four kids accompanying me?), and every time I entered another store, I left with more than what I intended to buy, often, significantly more.

And then one day, epiphany hit. We were in Store H, and the last item on the grocery list was at Store I, which had laundry detergent on sale (I make my own now, but that's for the next chapter). The Toddler was . . . acting like a toddler; the two oldest were skillfully manipulating my tired and distracted state; the four-year-old needed to use the bathroom, RIGHT NOW -- oh wait, he didn't need to use it anymore -- and I thought, forget it. I'll pick up the laundry detergent here, even though it's $1 more.

And I did. We stuffed everyone and the groceries back in the car, drove home, and called it a day, that is, after we unloaded everyone, carted in all the groceries, picked up the ones that fell out of the bags onto the cement driveway (pickles, in a glass jar, I believe), changed the four-year-old -- you know how this goes.

That night, when everyone was in bed but me and the Norwegian Artist, I thought about the laundry detergent. Yup, I paid $1 more for it, but I also didn't buy anything else at Store I. And then I realized, whenever I walk into a store, *even if I am only there to buy one thing*, I never leave without dropping at least $25.

Okay, so that sounds really simple and obvious, but when it comes to saving money, it's actually fairly profound. Maybe you have a willpower of steel, which is why your jeans are never too tight, but I don't, and when I walk into a store -- and nowadays I don't have those four noisy, chaotic, demanding, messy, lovable companions pointing out all of the colorful items that were arranged expressly to attract their notice -- it's hard not to say, "Hmm, that's a good deal; I'll pick up two," or "I forgot about peanut butter. Oh, and chocolate chips. And I really haven't treated myself to a magazine for a long time."

While it's true that we do forget things on our list, most of the time we can function without them until next week -- assuredly this is true about the chocolate chips, and the magazine's generally free at the library. If I don't see it, I don't buy it; and if I don't walk into the store in the first place, I don't see it.

So here's the weird idea that actually works: limit the number of stores you walk into each week. The dollar you would have saved by driving 6 miles to the next store (oops, there goes the dollar you saved) is rapidly consumed by the extra items you purchase, and if you don't see them, you don't buy them.

The money you save on understandable impulse buying can then be put aside for a more thoughtful, concerted purchase, one that will provide you with more pleasure, longer, than a jar of peanut butter.

Making Your Own Laundry Detergent

I have always disliked the laundry detergent aisle: it smells.

And while I know that multiple research teams have spent time and money figuring out how to attract me with those smells, coupled with loud garish packaging, the only tangible result in my life is that I sneeze.

Another result is that, if I buy the wrong box (I have no brand loyalty), assorted members of my family complain that their skin itches, or they're getting a rash.

For awhile, I bought the "unscented" version, which still smells, but I always baulked at the price. Laundry detergent is expensive.

But it doesn't have to be. Although there are labor intensive ways of making your own laundry detergent, involving stirring a series of ingredients together on the stovetop and pouring the whole conglomeration into a five gallon button, you can make a batch of laundry detergent in 15 minutes and not have to go anywhere near the stove.

You need these three things from the store:

- **Arm and Hammer Washing Soda** -- you'll find this in the laundry section of your grocery store. Mine is a 55 ounce box with the familiar Arm & Hammer logo of an arm wielding a hammer; the box is yellow or orange, and looks like a large version of the baking soda box (but it isn't baking soda, so don't use it that way!)

- **20 Mule Team Borax** -- also in the laundry section of your grocery store. White/grey box, 76 ounces. It might have a mule on the front, but mine just has some grassy meadow.

- **Fels Naptha Soap, one bar** -- you'll find this either in the laundry section or the soap section of your grocery store. Fels Naptha is a five-ounce bar of laundry soap, wrapped in white paper with red and green highlights. You can pretty much use any bar of natural soap -- free of excessive colors, aromas, and other additives -- that you want, and some people prefer Castile Soap, a glycerin bar, or Ivory brand soap.

The easiest way to see what you're looking for before you get to the store is to type the three ingredients into your Internet search engine and look at the images.

You will also need

- A fine cheese grater

- A container for the final product, something that easily holds three dry cups

- A one cup measurement

Measure out one cup of 20 Mule Team Borax and one cup of the Super Washing Soda and mix them in a bowl, or in the container that you're going to use as the final holder. Be aware that these two products are highly powdered, so you don't want to be so violent about your mixing them together that you send soda and borax dust throughout the air, into the room, and in your lungs. I generally put a cover on my container and shake the two up, or gently stir them together with a spoon.

Grab your Fels Naptha, the grater, and a bowl, and grate the bar, like cheese, into the bowl. I generally sit on the floor and do this, gently grating away and thinking -- this is one of those truly mindless jobs that allows me to daydream and hum.

Do use a fine grater -- if the pieces are too big, you'll have to rub them between your hands (I don't wear gloves, but you can if you feel that the soap will irritate them) until they're smaller. The grated soap doesn't have to be as finely powdered as the Borax and the soda, but you do want it as small as you can get it -- you don't want long shards of soap that look like grated Mozzarella cheese that you buy in a bag.

When the soap is all grated, mix it in with the soda/borax mixture until everything is well blended.

Your laundry soap is done.

To use it, mix 2-4 Tablespoons (experiment to see what works) with hot water to dissolve, then use as you would any liquid detergent.

When you run out, you've got plenty of soda and Borax left, and all you need to buy is another bar of soap.

How much money will this save you? I've seen some people, on some sites, announce that making your own laundry detergent -- something like this or its variations -- will cost you "pennies per load!" which is a variation on the "Live on $5 per day by Buying my Book!" theme.

Suffice it to say that the price of purchasing the Borax and washing soda, which will make multiple batches (there are 10 cups of powder in the 76-ounce box of Borax; a scant 7 cups in the 55-ounce box of washing soda) is significantly less than buying a bottle or box of detergent. The most expensive part of the homemade detergent package is the Fels Naptha soap, which I find for around $1.75.

I know that there are cheap, cheap detergents (they come in a brightly colored box that pretty much says, "Laundry Detergent" in bold black letters) that may factor out to pennies per load as well. I also know 1) how well my family's skin reacts to them and 2) I can't pronounce most of their ingredients. In case you haven't noticed throughout this book, I have a thing about being able to pronounce ingredients in the products that we eat or use.

Compared to name brands, making your own soap pays off big, because big names charge big prices. Compared also to specialty natural products, also, homemade costs far less. But if you feel that the more expensive products deserve the higher price because they do such a superior job, then stay with them, but why not try this? -- while you've still got a bit of your old detergent hanging around, make the homemade stuff, and compare the results. I've found them to be positive, which is why I continue to make, and use this product, but as with any suggestion in this book -- or from any other source -- do what's best for you and your family.

If you type "homemade laundry detergent" into your Internet search engine, you'll find all sorts of variations on this recipe, some of which will put you at the stovetop, stirring something in a big pot. I personally don't like standing at the stovetop, stirring things, which is why I stick to this particular recipe.

I will warn you -- if you've got something really, really dirty -- like with wine or tomato juice -- you may have to 1) wash the item more than once or 2) treat it with a pre-wash stain remover. Yep. I do that. I try not to touch the stuff; I know it's full of chemical junk; but sometimes it's the only way to get the massive amounts of ground-in food and dirt that a young child can grind into the front of her cute, cute blouse.

Pay No Attention to the Man Behind the Curtain

If you've never watched the 1939 version of the Wizard of Oz, do so. It's a classic of cinema that deserves a place in our collective consciousness, and while you're at it, check out the original book by L. Frank Baum, which, predictably, won't be the same as the movie. You can probably find both at your local library.

If you have seen the movie, you no doubt recognize the words in the title -- Dorothy and her friends, finally in the room with the great Oz himself, are initially frightened by the Wizard's huge face and booming voice floating in discombobulated state at the front of a long hall. But Toto, the clever dog, pushes aside a curtain to reveal a man wildly gesturing as he speaks Oz's words through a microphone.

Found out, he shuts the curtain, and the next words from the great wizard are, "Pay no attention to that man behind the curtain!"

It's one of my favorite lines, almost as good as the commercial with the white coated actor saying, "I'm not a doctor, but I play one on TV."

So what does this have to do with saving money? Just this, "Pay no attention to the ads stuffed inside your newspaper every week!"

Like the wizard, giving the impression that he is bigger and better and more powerful than he actually is, grocery ads give us the impression that food is cheaper and tastier and a much better buy than it actually is. If you cut out all the pictures of little boxes and bags and colorfully packaged items and stale cookies, you would be left with very little actual food.

And, as I mentioned in *Market Manipulation, Roast Chicken, and You*, there is a tendency within stores to nudge you into buying things you don't really need -- a free gallon of milk when you purchase two boxes of crackers you normally never eat, or "free" spaghetti sauce when you buy three packages of a name brand pasta product that is twice the price of the store brand.

Rarely are lemons on sale. Or onions. Flour, oil, sugar, butter, baking soda -- the basic with which you build made-from-scratch baked goods or meals -- are rarely, rarely in the ads. The more you learn to cook from basic ingredients, the less that you will find to attract you in the colorful pages of the weekly grocery ads, because you tend to stock up on basics.

Think about it -- processed food manufacturers, who churn out all sorts of food products that pretty much require ripping off the lid and dumping the contents into the microwave -- really need you to buy their stuff, and there's a lot competing for your attention. Sweet cereal with sugar bombs; Snackie Quackies with yellow cheese bits; artificially flavor-laden, gum thickened dip to slather on the Quackies -- much of what we spend our discretionary food money on tends to produce few nutrient benefits for the money, or the calories.

"But meat's on sale! and milk -- how will I know this if I don't check the ads?" Okay, so you may miss an item or two, but this savings will be made up for by your not buying all the other colorful items on the page. And as I mentioned in the chapter before this, *Saving Money in the Grocery Store -- One Weird, Workable Idea,* the fewer stores you enter, the less money you spend.

If you want to save money on groceries, focus on these strategies:

- Learn to cook

- Learn to cook

- Learn to cook

- Stock up on basic ingredients -- baking supplies like flour, sweeteners, leavens; vegetables and fruits; beans; peanut and nut butters; pastas and rice; eggs -- the more you learn to cook, the more that you will increase your supply of basic foods

- Shop once a month, if you can, for your basics that store well; you'll find that if you run out of a non-essential item, like chocolate chips, you can replace them with nuts, say, or coconut, and still have cookies without having to run to the store. No noodles? you've probably got rice, so just adjust the dish. Tuna out? poke through the fridge for leftover chicken. Use what you have in creative ways to keep from running to the store every day or two or three. Remember, every time you walk into a store, you will highly likely purchase three times as much as what you planned to get in the first place.

- Take advantage of holidays -- and grocery sales for holiday-themed foods -- to stock up. Baking products go on sale around Thanksgiving; hamburger is cheaper around Memorial Day, Father's Day, and the Fourth of July; Mexican-related food around Cinco de Mayo, you get the idea.

- Locally owned stores, not part of a chain, are not necessarily more expensive -- and they may be quite a bit cheaper. In our area, a little store named Andy's has the best produce and bulk food prices in the region; a small oriental market stocks the finest -- and least expensive -- curry paste, not to mention funky little coconut cookies from Thailand that finish off the meal just right. Find two or three stores that you really like and stick with them. I find that little tiny Andy's, and great big Cost-co warehouse foods, fill 80 percent of my food shopping needs, with the remainder taken up by Azure Standard, a healthy food cooperative based in Dufur, OR that meets all sorts of demands for whole and ancient grains, organic food, and natural products. (www.azurestandard.com)

- Remember to eat seasonally

- Don't be afraid of leftovers. There are actual people -- my grandparents were some of them -- who will not eat the same meal twice in succession. This used to drive my mother nuts, and no matter how she tried to disguise the meal, my grandparents wouldn't buy it. Hot roast beef sandwiches, the day after roast beef and mashed potatoes, did not fool them. (Oh, and in case you're wondering, this is the same grandmother who wouldn't wear a sweater over her gauzy blouse, preferring, instead, that the heat be turned up. She was a wonderful woman, but money was never a factor in her decisions.)

- Along the same lines, you don't have to eat something new and different every day. When it's summer, eat salads several days in succession; in the winter, make a big pot of soup and stretch it out. If it was good on Tuesday, it will be just as good, or even better, on Wednesday.

Eat More Like the Rest of the World

Before the Norwegian Artist and I embarked upon the adventure of parenthood, we lived in Colombia, South America for a year, and the experience changed the way we've thought about money, and the process of spending it, ever since.

One of the major thought-process changes was in how we view meat -- be it from a cow, pig, chicken, fish, goat, or lamb -- and if you're a vegan or vegetarian, this chapter won't be for you. But if you do eat meat products, one way of saving money on your food bill is to not eat quite so much of those meat products.

While that sounds stupidly obvious, stop, for a moment, and think about the "standard American dinner" -- a slab of meat; a starchy side dish like potatoes, noodles, or rice; and some sad, overcooked vegetable slathered with butter or ranch dressing to make it palatable. It's highly likely that there's more meat than vegetable on the plate, and meat isn't cheap.

Most of the world doesn't eat this way. Think about it:

- Spaghetti with sauce and vegetables, flavored with a little meat.

- Stir fried vegetables over rice and noodles, spices, and a little meat.

- Soup -- vegetables, rice/potatoes/noodles, lots of broth, a little meat.

- Beans, onions, peppers, tomatoes; a little meat, with a corn or flour tortilla.

- Lentils, onions, spices, tomatoes, a little meat, over rice.

In many of what we call "ethnic dishes," meat is a flavor component that dances and melds with many other ingredients to form a stew, curry, soup, casserole, or mixture that does not compartmentalize into three sections on the plate. Meat is there for texture, flavor, and interest, but it is not the star of the show -- and because you don't need so much of it, the overall dish made with it costs less.

If you are accustomed to meat-n-potatoes and very few veggies, then this will be an adjustment, but it's one worth making, because it's healthier not only for your pocketbook but for your overall health as well -- there's no argument that Americans, especially, could strongly do with more vegetables, fruit, and other high fiber elements in their diet.

Throughout the years, I have informally watched people and their eating habits, and I've noticed that those diners, especially children, who eat the standard meat/starch/vegetable American meal tend to be pickier in their eating habits than people who consume their food jumbled together in soups, stews, and cassoulets. Choosey eaters are not only exasperating to be around, they're also more expensive, since their limited tastes mean that you have to supply what they'll eat, regardless of whether it's in season or reasonably priced.

177

Of course, you don't want to put your family into system shock, and if you make too many changes, too fast, you may drive people out of the kitchen and into the drive-in, but if you're the cook in the house, you've got major say, control, and power.

One night this week, make something that doesn't divide neatly into three. Pair it with something familiar, like bread or a banana, so if somebody at the table absolutely hates it, he or she won't starve. But insist that this person -- who, incidentally, may be an adult, not a child -- give it a try, and announce that next week, you will repeat your experiment with a different kind of food.

Cooking has the huge potential to be an extremely fun thing to do, and it's relatively cheap to experiment. Have fun with your food.

Kitchen Failures -- Sometimes They're Delicious

As you progress in your journey of either learning to cook or experimenting with different foods, you will no doubt encounter a . . . failure or two. Sometimes, despite following the recipe, what we make just doesn't turn out to our expectations, either because our expectations were too high, the recipe wasn't as good as what it promised, or our skills weren't quite up to our ambitions.

While it's tempting to toss whatever it is we've made out, food is food, and if it's possible to recycle it into something edible, it's worth trying. If you're worried about what the guests will say, put the failure in the fridge for another day when they're not there; I've found that my family members can yell away all they want, and I can be remarkably impervious to their cries.

One weekend, the Son and Heir was indescribably excited about making Gjetost (yay-toast), a Norwegian "cheese" produced by simmering whey for 12 hours until it reduces to a creamy, caramelized concoction. Norwegian children apparently eat it spread on their breakfast toast.

Maybe it was the terms "creamy" and "caramelized" that fooled the Son and Heir into thinking that this highly ethnic dish -- which the recipe mentioned one acquires a taste for (that's always a warning sign) -- would be delectably different.

179

Well, it was different all right, and our first thought upon tasting it was, "Those poor Norwegian children," and the second thought, mine, was,

"All that time and anticipation is not going to waste. We are eating this stuff -- not on toast! -- somehow." (You mothers understand this, I know. Our children are always our little cherubs, and their sad faces -- even when they're covered with beard stubble -- spur us to action.)

"I don't know, Mom," the Son and Heir dejectedly replied. "This looks like a failure to me."

"Kitchen failures are opportunities, son," I replied. "And this is a greater opportunity than most."

I made pizza, topping a Kamut flour crust with mozzarella cheese, roasted bell pepper, caramelized onions, garlic, and -- shredded Gjetost. Even Small Person, our three-year-old grandchild, ate her portion, although, admittedly, that was after we told her she couldn't have dessert until she did. But it was excellent pizza, really, and the unique salty flavor of the Norwegian product complemented the rest of the toppings. (By the way, the Norwegian Artist had no choice about eating the pizza, whether or not he wanted dessert, because he's Norwegian after all, and this is in his heritage. If he has a problem with that, he can always take it up with his mother.)

The next day, Gjetost transformed dull, boring bean soup into *Wow! This is really Norwegian!* fare with its husky, deep, complex personality, and we all agreed that we'll make it through the rest of the stuff yet, especially since it looks like it has a shelf life of 25 years.

The point of all this is not to urge you to flip past the page about Gjetost in your new cheese book -- although I would encourage you to consider doing so -- but rather, to reassure you that seemingly failed kitchen experiments can rise up out of the ashes (sometimes, if you've baked something too long, there are literal ashes, by the way) to a new, different, intriguing, and mildly edible concoction.

The very worst thing that can happen is that the dog will get an extra portion at dinner. Well, okay, the very worst thing is that the dog will refuse the extra portion and the compost pile will be enhanced, but worms eat anything, don't they?

But the best thing that can happen is that you will have experimented -- several times -- and wound up with something edible, maybe even tasty, and you will have survived. And you'll keep experimenting and trying new things, and each time you do, you'll get more and more adventurous, and better and better about what you create, and increasingly versatile about what you eat.

You may not be invited to a lot of potlucks, but you'll be able to eat anything at any of them once you get there.

Children Are Expensive

I don't read newspapers any more, but when I did, every three weeks or so there was a feature article on children, and how expensive they were to raise. The latest amount seems to be around $250,000 to raise each child to adulthood, which means that, somehow, the Norwegian Artist and I have come up with a million dollars in change lying around the house and rattling around in the washing machine.

Odd. It never seemed like we had that kind of money.

The first thing to do with these articles is to ignore them, or use the paper they're printed on to start a fire in the woodstove, because all they do is engender fear and anxiety, without really solving any problems or offering any tangible, useful advice. If you don't have kids, they'll discourage you from having them; if you do have kids, you'll stay awake at night fearing that there's no way you'll get them to adulthood.

If you do have kids, however, it's no surprise that they cost money, but there are things you can do to mitigate this.

First and foremost, do not allow your children to dictate what you buy for them, and how much, based upon pressure and guilt feelings -- it really doesn't matter what other parents are doing out there; it matters what you're doing. It also doesn't matter how old your kids are -- if they're really really young, and the only girl without a pink princess battery operated Barbie car, then you'll be tempted to flagellate yourself -- but don't. It will not irretrievably harm your daughter if she grows up without a pink Barbie car. . (All three of my daughters are just fine.)

When she's ten, and the only one at school without the latest cell phone (which the school prohibits being used during school hours), she'll make sure to let you know how old fashioned and uncaring you are, but if you don't see a valid reason for her to possess an expensive digital item when she can't pick her socks up off the bedroom floor, then hold your ground.

At 16, she may be expecting a real car -- not pink -- because all of her friends receive cars for their 16th birthday. You know that old saying, "If all your friends were jumping off a cliff, would you do so too?" -- it applies to us adults as much as kids.

Of course, if you yourself are concerned about what other people buy, how other people live, and what other people think of you, or what other kids think of your kids -- then you don't have much counterargument to help you out.

It does not have to be this way. While peer pressure is strong, and media influence is stronger, you can stand tall and be honest with your kids from the very beginning, explaining why you do what you do, and why you won't give in to this demand, but will make allowances for that one.

And speaking of allowances, we always found that a nominal amount (because we never have had a lot to spare) given to a child based upon his age and maturity to be a useful leverage tool. Once, when our oldest was 8, we were in the grocery store when she announced that we should buy drinking straws.

"We don't need straws," I replied.

"Yes, we do -- it's so much more fun to drink when we have straws. I WANT straws!"

This had the potential to escalate fast. Out of the corner of my eye I saw an older couple stop and watch. I thought for a moment.

"You get an allowance," I finally said. "And it's enough to purchase straws. If you want the straws, by all means get them. You're free to do so."

In her court. She didn't miss a beat.

"I won't get them then," she said. "They're not worth spending my money on."

As we progressed down the aisle, the older couple approached me and smiled.

"Good job," the man said. "I was wondering how you were going to handle that."

Of course, it's easier to deal with an 8-year-old than a teenager, but by the time the kids get older, you've had that many more years to practice. When our second daughter was 15, she decided she needed clothes, new clothes, and more of them than I was prepared to buy or able to afford. So I came up with a number that I thought was reasonable and told her that she had that amount to work with for her clothing allowance that year.

"You can spend it all on three pairs of designer shoes," I said, "but there's no more until next year."

She took it on as a challenge, sat down and listed out what she needed versus what she wanted, and stretched the amount out over the next several months. She shopped heavily in second hand stores, learned to accessorize, and contented herself with two variations of one item when she earlier would have demanded six. All of a sudden, name brands and the latest looks didn't matter so much anymore, and as she slowly added to her wardrobe, she added a sense of pride to her sense of style.

Of course, she made a few unwise purchases, but it didn't take many of those for her to learn that a finite amount of money, indiscriminately spent, didn't buy what she needed or wanted.

Yes, children cost money -- they do eat, after all. But they do not have to be a raging expense, demanding the latest gadget or item of clothing because it's in and everyone else has it. If we as adults are choosing to no longer live under this tyranny of marketing control, then we can give our children the gift of independence by telling them no, explaining our reasons, and standing our grounds.

It's not easy. Nothing about raising children is "easy."

But it's worth it, because not only do we save money better spent elsewhere, we also train up a next generation to be sensible about its purchases, willing to wait and defer gratification, and to live contentedly with what it has.

As the old saying goes, the best way we teach is by example, and if we ourselves pursue the newest gadget, the latest fad, the most recently released movie, simply because we achieve a sense of contentment by spending, then this is what we will pass on to our kids.

Really, we can do better than that -- not only for them, but for us.

In 32 Seconds Your Life Can Change

While we're on the subject of children, this might be a good time to mention that they grow up fast, and if you're in the midst of having them and your house is constantly messy and they're nagging you all the time for this and that and you never have enough time to get done with all the money-saving and money-making projects you want to accomplish (feeling overwhelmed? This might be a good time to re-read *Overwhelmed Is Not the New Normal*) -- they won't be around forever.

Nothing on this earth lasts forever, although some things -- meetings come immediately to mind -- seem as if they do. As a society we compensate for too many claims on our time, fit within too little of that time, by multi-tasking, something that American women with children, especially, have elevated to an art form.

Most of this multi-tasking is mental, in that while you're washing the dishes and refereeing an argument at the breakfast table, you're thinking, "I'll get those bills paid later this morning, after starting a load of laundry. A couple birthdays coming up -- I'd better get some ideas going. Oops -- smells like someone needs to be changed."

If you're working outside the home, the dishes, laundry, bills, birthdays and arguments will be waiting for you in the evening, not to mention the person who needs to be changed, although it is sincerely hoped that this particular afternoon project was cared for.

Rarely are you living precisely in the present, and the more children in the house and the younger they are, the more tasks there are to process. Before you know it, ten years have gone by, many of those children have driver's licenses, and you've developed this distressing habit of living in the future. Now, in addition to the bills, laundry, dishes, birthdays -- but not necessarily diaper changing -- you think,

"Everyone's growing up. Soon we'll be all alone. How will I deal with this?"

Are you there yet? I am.

Popularly, it's called Empty Nest Syndrome; supposedly, women worldwide welcome this liberation from the noise and chaos of children in the house; in real life, I suspect most people hate it as much as I do.

But one thing it's teaching me, before it's too late, is to stop mentally multi-tasking and force myself to be in the present, full time, fully engaged, and without a thought to the future, because none of us know, or can control, what happens within the next 32 seconds, much less five minutes, week, months, or years from now.

By the time you finish this article, your life could have radically changed -- and you may not even know it. Good or bad, often in between, life's circumstances happen continuously. Because we're human and intelligent, reasonable beings, we plan for the future constantly, and while it is admirable to do so, it's wise to recognize that the future is ultimately unknown to us. There can be a lot of twists and turns in our road that force us to reevaluate our financial, familial, social, educational, and lifestyle goals, but as long as we remain flexible about this concept, we'll be all right.

This hit me between the eyes when The Norwegian Artist and I were discussing Small One, our granddaughter, and her upcoming fourth birthday.

"I wonder what she'll be like when she's 17?" the Norwegian mused.

How could we possibly know? I thought. And if we can't foresee 13 years into the future, why do we live our lives as if we could? Year after year of moving from one project to the next, planning out two chores ahead while I'm in the midst of another one, has trained me to never stop and fully be in the present, a significant chunk of which is now in the past. And looking backwards, I don't remember the laundry, the dishes, the bills, the chores -- I remember the people, many of whom are still in my life today, just not the way they were 10 years ago.

Yesterday, I sat on the porch, soaking up the sun, with a kitty on my left, my knitting in my lap, and Tired of Being Youngest to my right. Initially, my thoughts raced on about TBY and how quickly she was growing, and how quickly she would be gone. I assure you, that's a good way to turn a sunny day into a dark one.

So I stopped. Pet the cat (she's long haired, and has dreadful mats), put down my knitting, and turned to Tired of Being Youngest.

"Do you want me to help you study for your quiz?" I asked.

189

She looked up, surprised. Usually I'm too busy to do this kind of stuff.

"You bet!"

For 45 minutes, we companionably discussed the different kinds of fruit -- melons, pomes, berries, pitted -- and gently chatted and laughed.

I thought to myself, "Isn't this what we're reaching for, when we seek the good life?" --companionship, time with the people we love, time -- period -- to think and wonder and daydream. These are the things that we can't buy but which we can enjoy -- as long as we are open to seeing the opportunities when they arise.

I don't know where Tired of Being Youngest, or I, will be 3 years from now, or 3 months from now, or 32 seconds from now, but that afternoon, we were together -- and I was there, in the present, soaking up each moment as my skin soaked up the sun.

It was warm and delicious.

You Don't Have to Do This All by Yourself, You Know

Saving money takes time -- cooking for yourself instead of buying ready made, repairing a broken item as opposed to replacing it with a new one, learning and perfecting a new skill which will save or make income later.

Logic tells us that we can't add a bunch of new tasks or activities to our life without subtracting others -- those others hopefully not being sleep or time to sit and eat a leisurely meal -- and as you make changes in your lifestyle to reflect a less consuming, more creating philosophy, remember the other members in your household. Call upon them to help. It is not up to you, singlehandedly, to turn your family's finances and lifestyle around.

Stop right there, you say -- "I'm single. There are no other members in my household."

Okay, so that's a good thing, and a bad one -- it's good because you're the one calling all the shots in your household, and if you determine that Project A needs to be done before Project B, then you don't have to go through a committee to make it so. That saves time and headaches.

It's a bad thing because, if you had even one other person in your household, he or she could be working on Project B while you're working on Project A. BUT -- if you relax about Project B and give yourself a break on it while you're working on Project A, you won't drive yourself nuts. Be realistic about what you can accomplish, and don't heap projects and expectations on yourself.

Think, also, of the other people in your life who aren't necessarily in your household -- can they help? Let's say that you want to make soap and you've never done it before -- do you know someone who does, and even better, has all the necessary ingredients for doing so? Then call this person, and connect. You may find a soap-making companion who will join with you on other adventures, thereby splitting and lightening your load as you seek to make changes in your life.

For those of you whose household consists of more than one person, recognize that you do not have to approach the changes you are trying to make as if you were the only one who benefits from making them.

And so, we come to the concept of chores, a word that brings to mind milking cows or pitching hay, but really just means pitching in to do whatever needs to be done to keep the household -- whether that household is on a 20-acre farm or in a downtown apartment -- going.

When I was a young child, my one and only chore was to feed the cat -- because my mother did pretty much everything else, and although she needed help from the rest of us, she didn't want it. So she didn't get it.

She almost didn't get the cat fed -- not only because I hate the greasy feeling that gets on your hands when you touch the cat food, but because I didn't feel especially needed even in this little task. If I didn't do it -- and I frequently didn't -- mom did.

Things were different with our own kids. Maybe it's because I am from a different generation, but I never felt, as my mom did, that it was my job as the woman of the household to do all of the cleaning, washing, cooking, vacuuming, mending, sewing, and toilet swishing, and I really did like to sit down with a book before 11 o'clock at night.

So we all worked together. For the longest time, I was the chief cook, for no other reason than that the average 8-year-old isn't much of a chef, but as the kids grew older, they learned to do more and more in the kitchen, until as teenagers one of them could take the meal for the night and I would do something else -- wash the dishes, say. Another child dried (we wash our dishes by hand, incidentally, never having invested in a dishwasher appliance; some people clean their dishes so thoroughly before stacking them in, I've always wondered why they needed the machine); another folded clothes; still another tidied the house. The Norwegian Artist cleared the table or swept the floor or picked up towels -- which in a household of four children is pretty much a fulltime occupation -- the jobs varied, but the only rule was, "If Mom and Dad are working, everyone's working."

193

Because we started when the children were very, very young, doing chores together was a normal facet of life, and if anyone balked at doing his or her part, there were plenty of other household members -- primarily siblings -- who made sure that they didn't get away with it. (Our second daughter's subtle technique was to disappear into the bathroom as soon as the meal was being cleared, but we all -- especially her older sister -- noticed this regular absence, and made sure to save her job aside. When the youngest child conceived this notion of indefinite bathroom breaks years later, we were all trained to identify and eliminate this technique. The second daughter was especially vigilant.)

But people rarely balked, because, unlike me when I was designated to feed the cat, each member of the family knew for certain that he or she was needed. After all, if the person drying the dishes didn't do so, the dishes didn't get dried, because everyone else was busy washing the dishes, or sweeping the floor, or even feeding the cat. Being needed is a powerful incentive, and while it's tempting -- often as the woman of the house -- to feel that you should take all of the unpleasant chores into your own hands, do not rob the other household members, especially your children, of this experience.

When we entertain guests -- regardless of their age -- we can tell who is used to helping out in their home, and who is not, because when we all get up from the table, the helping people do just that -- they help. If we insist that they sit and relax, many still hang around, picking up a dish here, grabbing a rag there, or standing at the kitchen counter, keeping the dish washer company. These are genuinely fun people to be around.

Your new lifestyle -- creating more, consuming less -- takes time, but if you parcel that time wisely around the household members, you won't be just getting the chores out of the way, you'll be interacting and working with one another. While it's true that you're not bowling or watching a movie or splashing in the water park, not all together time has to be recreational. Indeed, it is our working time together that draws us closer, because we accomplish as a family group so much more than we can do alone.

This week, focus on not doing it all yourself. Ask for and incorporate the help of other family members, and do not feel guilty about this. You're a family. You work as a unit. If this seems unusual, it's because our modern society fractures that unit -- sending one child to a basketball game here, another child to watch TV in his room, your spouse out to the garage, and you in the kitchen with the dishes and the dirty floor and the laundry and the cooking.

You are walking a new, different path -- one not only of spending less and saving more, but of slowing down to enjoy the life you have been given. So much of that enjoyment comes from time together, and time is not something that can be bought. Incrementally, your daily life and your household will incorporate changes from the money-saving habits you develop, and if you relax about this and flow with what works for you, you and your family will start to look very different from the society surrounding you.

And what does the society around you look like? Well, it focuses on money as a means of purchasing happiness, or at least as a means of showing the people around us that we're successful because we're rich.

Deep down, we know that money isn't the true indicator of success in life -- after all, we all smile, knowingly, at the saying,

"Nobody ever regretted on his death bed that he didn't spend more time at work."

If we know this deep down, then let's practice it daily, and not fret about how we're looking different from everyone else. You'll be surprised -- people will come up to you at random times and say things along the lines of,

"You seem so happy and content with what you have. How do you do that?"

And of course you'll answer, "Because I bought Carolyn Henderson's book, *Live Happily on Less*."

Life Doesn't Match

We have some friends who were newlyweds in the 1970s.

Now I don't know if you know anything about the 70s -- if you've lived through them it's hard to forget -- but the decade is not known for its exquisite taste and style. Avocado green appliances, mustard yellow shag carpet, orange wide-flared bell bottom pants, loud polyester floral fabric -- even typing it out is painful.

But back then, this was style, and our friends, who are very stylish, outfitted their rental apartment with all new furniture: Brown/lime green/yellow plaid couches and chairs, the aforementioned shag carpet, the atrociously hued kitchen stove and refrigerator.

It all matched; it was very expensive; and they charged it.

Fortunately for the rest of us, maybe not so fortunately for our friends, styles change, and before the charge card was halfway paid off, the brand new furniture was out of date and recognized for what it was -- really, really ugly.

So, they went out and bought new stuff.

And again, before the charge card was paid off, that furniture was out of date.

This cycle is endless, but if you choose not to jump on the merry go round in the first place, you don't have to have a credit card balance that never goes away, and you can still have a house that looks nice -- it just doesn't match.

Our own house is an eclectic mix of new furniture that we saved up and purchased for our 25th anniversary, only two years later than the actual anniversary; used items from family members and second hand stores; a rotating supply of paintings by Steve Henderson, my Norwegian Artist; and accessorizing elements -- pillows I've made, shawls I've knitted, quilt runners I've sewn. This last is especially fun because I've been able to combine my hobbies (*Create*, earlier in this book) with home decor to pull together something unique and special to us.

When we sit in our living room, we are less concerned with what guests will think (and if they're highly critical of who and what we are, they probably won't be in our house in the first place) than that we are comfortable here, and we are surrounded by items that mean something to us.

Interestingly, the new furniture we purchased -- leather couch, chair, glider rocker, dining room table -- isn't holding up so well, because most mid-grade furniture is designed to look really nice on the showroom floor, but not hold up to daily use. Although the table is sturdy and made with solid wood, the lacquer finish is cheap, showing up a changing array of mystery stains. The dark coffee leather couch is actually tan, evidenced by the color that shows underneath the wear marks. The leather on the chair's headrest split open and peeled away, artfully covered by a lace shawl.

The best looking piece of furniture in the house is what we call the Dead Cat Table, so named because years ago in my childhood one of the cats died on top of it. An antique that my mother picked up back when antiques were considered junk, it wears its scratches well, and the hinges still work.

Given the quality of much of what is in the furniture store, it's not such a bad idea to scour the second hand stores -- some of what is there is of better quality than what you can buy new, and that which is of the same quality already has the scratches and dents that your new purchase will get within the first six months of its life in your house.

The primary purpose of furniture is to provide us a place to sit, eat, or store things, and if you're not worried about everything 1) being brand new and 2) matching, you can mix and match and create an environment that works for you and your budget.

Our oldest daughter, Eldest Supreme, is a diva at pulling together stylish interiors on an extreme budget, and she regularly stops by two or three local second hand stores to see what's new. An old lamp table, covered with bright fabric, sets her back less than $10, yet gives a whole new look to the room. When she wants to renovate, she moves the table to a different spot and covers it with a different piece of fabric. Pillows, a couple plants, an unusual vase (extra cheap because it has a crack along the side, but she arranges it with the crack against the wall), and a throw rug complete the look for under $25. When she's bored, she replaces the accessories.

She loves where she lives -- and how she lives -- because it reflects her savvy purchasing habits, and her living space is uniquely her own.

This week -- renovate your living space by moving the furniture around. Poke through your closets and see if you've got old pillows or material hanging around that you can toss, drape, and accessorize with. If you want something new, take a trip to the second hand store and limit yourself to $10 -- see what you can do. Whatever it is that you purchase, it will likely become a mental focal point for you, and a great basis for a story that you can pass on to your family and friends!

Never Say No to Free

I don't like "Never do this" phrases and use them sparingly, but "Never -- or at least, most of the time -- say no to anything free" is good advice.

Of course, you don't want to become subject matter for a hoarders reality show, and if you've got so much stuff hanging around that you're renting a storage unit you probably want to ignore this particular piece of advice, but for the most part, let people know that you're willing to consider their cast offs.

Not their garbage, mind you -- broken, rotting, sagging, unusable, city-dump fare -- but furniture they're passing on (possibly because they've bought, and charged, all new, matching stuff), dishes, clothes (of a size that fits someone in your household), games and puzzles, craft supplies, appliances (if they work, and you need them). Your goal is not to be a replacement for the landfill but to meet your needs on a low-cost or free basis by using items that other people want to get rid of.

You know, one man's trash is another man's treasure. You're that other man.

And speaking of men, the Norwegian Artist has a different list of things he considers -- wood for building or burning (we heat our house with a wood stove); hand or garden tools -- even if the handle's broken -- because he usually has spare handles hanging around; PVC pipe; plastic sheeting; old windows; doors; even a kitchen sink -- while we were building our house, we lived in a renovated barn, and the 1940s kitchen sink that we installed in our temporary home is still there, now serving as the sink for the Norwegian's art studio.

You don't have to say yes to everything that's offered to you, but the more open that you are to offers, the more you will receive them. Many people are reluctant to offer because they think you'll be offended. Don't be offended.

Sometimes, when you are offered free items, they come as a package deal, meaning that you'll get some things you want along with others that you don't. If you can handle what it is you don't want -- meaning that you can throw it away or pass it on without incurring a charge -- then take it and get rid of it when the giver is gone. Some people are simply incapable of throwing things away, and consider it part of your gift in life that you can do this (More on this in the next chapter, *Living Green? Don't Be Weird about It.)*

Years ago, when the children were young, someone offered us an old swing set. We took it, and through the years, it continued to fall apart, until there was only one swing left. But by that time, the kids were using it for a pull-up bar, or they would simply hang on the top bar and swing, or they climbed over it. Later, when everyone was adult sized, the Norwegian Artist dismantled it and used the metal poles in the garden. That swing set earned its final rest, the kids got all of the play out of it that they needed, and we hadn't spent a thing.

This week, be open to offers for free items; if your friends or family are cleaning out their garage or talking about taking a load to the second hand store, ask them what they've got and see if it will fit into what you need. No, it won't be new, but if you went to the store and bought the item new, brought it home and started using it, it wouldn't be new after the first day either.

That initial rush we all get when we buy something -- whether it's a new sofa or a package of socks -- doesn't last forever. Sometimes, we can get that same rush by accepting something that's free, that's in reasonably good condition, and that fulfills a need -- with the extra rush that we didn't pay anything for it.

An nowadays, with the emphasis on reduce/reuse/recycle, we can tell ourselves that we're being earth friendly in addition to financially wise. Green isn't just the color of money.

Living Green? Don't Be Weird about It

While I rarely involve myself in groupie things, I participate now and then when the reason is right. This particular event was an ad hoc assemblage of women, fabric, and sewing machines churning out shorts and shirts and knitted caps for babies on another continent.

At the end of the day, the leader approached me with a black garbage sack full of scraps, the largest of which was half the size of a toilet paper square.

"None of us can use these, but we just can't bear to throw them away.

"I know you quilt. Maybe you could make a project out of these?"

Easy answer.

"Of course I can."

I took the bag home and did what 19 other quilters in the room could not do: I threw it away. This is my gift -- I mentioned it in the last chapter, *Never Say No to Free*, and because I am able to throw things away when I don't need them, I am offered lots of things, some of which I use, and some of which I throw away. It's a good gift to cultivate.

I know you're concerned, but don't be. My inner green girl was fine: she recognizes a bag of trash when she sees it, and it's beyond even my obsessive nature to piece a king-sized bedspread with fraying clumps of crumpled cloth French kissed by dust bunnies and entwined with bent straight pins.

Which is not to say that I don't reduce, reuse, recycle, or, as the generation before me put it, use it up, wear it out, make it do, or do without. My brother laughs at my "chicken" pie, which consists mainly of meat scraps from the boiled carcass, rounded out with lots of onions (cheap), potatoes (cheap), carrots (cheap), and celery (cheap). The ratio of vegetal matter to meat would make the food pyramid people (oh wait now, it's a plate this week, isn't it?) swoon.

One holiday weekend, I embarked on a knitted junk hat, a simple confection of leftover yarn from earlier projects, because when the stash grows beyond two shoeboxes full I feel dissipated and dissolute. So, surrounded by the most important things in my life – my tribe – I knit during the off moments, enjoying sibling squabbling and chaotic serenity.

One yarn – merino wool and cashmere – I bought on vacation years ago; another, camel blended with mohair, returned from a business trip; alpaca spooning with silk evoked memories of a weekend at College Girl's lair – I unashamedly and unabashedly go for the good stuff, and I wear what I make out of it.

What's left over goes into the plastic shoe box, and when the lid doesn't snap shut, I knit chicken pie, but seriously, the yarn pieces need to be more than two feet in length. Enough of neurotic already.

It's okay, at some point, to call junk what it is – trash – and throw it away. I recognize that many times, it may be another man's (or quilter's) treasure, but sometimes, seriously, it's truly garbage, and the effort of packaging it, storing it, and worrying about what to do with it, outweighs the benefits of stuffing a pillow with it. Despite the wisdom of middle age, I have not found a certifiably constructive use for old toilet paper rolls, and there are only so many long cords to be contained by a cardboard tube.

We all have a lot of stuff, too much, admittedly, but rather than reprimanding and rebuking one another into a lifestyle of fanatical austerity, why not live in reality? We can use up what we've got, pass it on to someone else if we don't need it (as long as it isn't a black garbage bag of snippets), purchase what we require, indulge in what we desire (yak yarn!) and be thankful for it all.

So we buy things, wisely, for ourselves and others, and enjoy them with gratitude – the same way we enjoy Thanksgiving turkey, the stuffing, the mashed potatoes, the pie. The next day, we eat leftovers, make soup from what's left after that, bless the kitties on the porch with the giblets.

I mean, somebody has to eat those things.

The Economics of Stuff

There's an important thing to remember about saving money: it's easy to become cheap.

"Cheap" is not a word with positive connotations, and there's a reason for that -- cheap people think small, grasping for every penny, so concentrated on saving money that they forget about the people around them. Hand in hand with saving money should be the concept of generosity -- even the poorest among us in this country has a significant amount of stuff, far more stuff than the poorest in many third world countries. Very few of us go to bed having eaten only one meal during the day.

In our college days, we frequented the yard sales, filling our rented hut with others' cast offs that managed to light our living room, cover the stains on the carpet, and provide reading material for our imaginary free time. Not having a use for cute glass animals that used to hold cheap perfume, we passed on those.

To get the good stuff, you had to arrive early, or else all that was left were the aforementioned penguins with party hats for lids. But even getting there early wasn't enough sometimes, chiefly because of a beak-nosed, sharp-eyed old dame who swooped on anything decent like a hawk dives for a mouse.

This woman was scary. She was also the manager of The Happy Pleasant Place, a little store on Main Street that raised money for the senior center. And judging from the prices of the merchandise at the Happy Pleasant Place, the manager's primary goal was to make money, lots of it.

Small, wiry, and wearing a perpetual scowl, the Scary Woman finagled her way in early -- sometimes hours early -- to the best sales. Whether she cast a spell on the homeowners or simply relied upon the threat of her scowl, she swept through the wares like a tropical storm, grasping and clutching at anything that wasn't ticky tacky glassware.

Each week's haul she bore to The Happy Pleasant Place, which might have been more aptly named Dragon's Lair, and trebled, quadrupled, and octupled the prices. For awhile this worked, and The Happy Pleasant Place thrived.

But rumors fly in a small town, and it didn't take long before people realized that the Wicked Witch of the West who was wrenching Dorothy's shoes off her feet was the same person trying to sell the Ruby Slippers for four times their value at The Happy Pleasant Place. I don't know, maybe some people didn't like wandering into the shop and finding their first set of dishes, which they had marked significantly down at their yard sale because they thought it could go to some college student, selling for the same amount they paid for a new set at a high-end department store.

Over the next few months, fewer and fewer people frequented The Happy Pleasant Place, and eventually it closed its doors altogether. While this may have made some people sad, we were ecstatic to find the yard sales safe places to attend again, and we were actually able to pick up a set of plastic dishes for a price that we could afford.

(So excited were we about this find, that we started discussing the possibilities of tracking down food to serve on the plates.)

Nowadays, the scary yard sale woman wouldn't bother with the storefront, opting, instead, to post everything online in auction format. I know individuals who do this, and for the most part, they are terrific people.

But the same grasping attitude of buying good stuff cheaply and selling it dearly prevails, with the justification being, "If they don't know they've got a Van Gogh here, that's just their problem."

Fine. I see that. Making a profit is the American Way.

But so also is generosity, and in the past, many people set out their used items in yard sales at drastically reduced prices, with the tacit agreement between merchant and buyer: "I'm cleaning up my house; and you're getting a good deal." The merchant had the added bonus of knowing that he was helping out a fellow human being.

Because we don't like marking tiny red dots with prices like 10 cents or a quarter and sticking them to items that we no longer need, we tend to skip putting on yard sales altogether and simply box up the items to give away. Sure, we could use the extra cash, but like most Americans, we've got a lot of stuff, and it's worth more than money to pass on what we don't need to someone who is doing without.

If you have extra stuff that you don't need, think twice before you organize a yard sale and spend hours marking little red dots. Are there people you know who could use what you have? (Possibly, is some of this stuff another man's treasure that was passed on to you?)

In addition to choosing to live outside the norm financially, Steve, my Norwegian Artist, and I opted to homeschool our kids (two out of four which we had at home, but that's another story for another book). The homeschooling community is an intriguing place, populated by a lot of families with one breadwinner between them, either one person doing it all or both of them splitting a part-time job.

Obviously, this is done so that someone is home to school the kids.

But what this means is that there is no double income, and nowadays, a double income is pretty much thought of as a necessity to live a normal American life. So on a single income, these families -- many of which are bigger than the norm, whatever the norm is -- function. There's not a lot of extra money floating about.

But some of that money, extra or not, goes toward purchasing school books for the children, with the expectation that, after child number one has used the math book, child number two will use it a few years later, then child number three, and so on. The families wisely get the most out of their purchase.

That's great. That's what we did, and it's sensible.

The problem arose after the last child was done with the book. In our own home, we figured that four kids had benefited (maybe that's not the word they would use) from this resource, and we had definitely gotten our money's worth. So we found someone who needed the book and gave it to them.

But we were, once again, oddities in the room.

Far too many families sold their used books, with the reasoning that they needed the money, and they were selling it for a "used price" anyway. We know some families who practically wrapped the book in plastic wrap while it was being used so that it would be in pristine condition, ten years later, for resale.

People, this is cheap. I know, I know -- you're being a wise steward of your finances; textbooks are expensive; and the buyer is getting a better deal than buying new. But I found, repeatedly, that the people who sold their books like this had an inflexible, grasping, selfish attitude about money.

By gosh, they just never had enough -- and yet many of them were fairly well off, single income speaking. They had enough food, their kids dressed well and fashionably, their cars were under 10 years old, they had the requisite number of TVs and computers and cell phones -- they pretty much looked, and lived, like double income families.

And a surprising number called themselves Christians.

And yet, when it came to giving away something that they had more than received their purchase price for, they just couldn't do it. It meant so much to them that they received back -- after years of use -- at least half of what they had paid for the resource in the first place. This, they were convinced, was a wise stewardship of their finances.

But wise stewardship of your finances, my friend, is more than saving money.

If you have been blessed with enough to eat, decent clothes to wear, and a roof over your head, then you have more than a big chunk of the world. When you find that you have extra, or that you no longer need an item that you have put to good use, why not give it to someone?

Giving is as much a part of living a wise financial life as saving money is. It is a tangible reminder that there is always someone out there who has less than we do, and it is in our power to bless their lives by giving, freely, from the abundance in ours.

Give.

It feels good.

Life is tough; finances are tight; jobs are scarce.

We need each other.

Thank You

Well, we're done. Fifty-two chapters, or fifty-two weeks, pass quickly, and whether you read this book in one sitting or savored being around me for a full year, I hope that something I said helped.

I want to leave you with a few thoughts:

- This is your life, your family, and your journey. Find what works for you, and don't worry about the stuff that doesn't, even if other people rave about it.

- Take your time, and be patient with change. As I said in the introduction, saving money is more of a mindset and a lifestyle than it is a series of quick, fast, dirty tricks.

- That being said, one quick, fast, dirty trick to saving money is to walk away from any book, DVD, or seminar that promises easy, EASY ways to save lots and lots of money. Have you ever seen a mmu mmu? It's a one-size fits all dress that looks like a big fabric bag. There are no one-size-fits-all solutions to any of life's issues.

- Enjoy life, and be grateful for it. Your next breath is not something that you, or anybody, can buy. It's a gift.

And I'd like to ask you something: if you enjoyed this book, will you please let others know? I am self-published, and I depend upon the good word of good people to pass me on. If you're the type of person who writes reviews, I wouldn't mind some happy stars on the Amazon reviews page for this book.

If you want to read more of me, here are a few places to look:

Grammar Despair: Quick, simple solutions to problems like, "Do I say him and me or he and I?" (Paperback book and Kindle digital; available through Amazon.com and other online book distributors) Don't let the word "grammar" chase you away -- I wrote this book specifically for people who want or need to write, don't want to sound like an idiot doing it, and are not interested in diagramming sentences or learning the difference between a subordinate and insubordinate clause. You have something to say -- and I want to help you feel confident in saying it.

Life Is a Gift (Kindle digital book of 30 lifestyle essays and 30 art images by my Norwegian Artist, Steve Henderson. Available at Amazon.com)

The Jane Austen Driving School (Second Kindle digital book of 30 lifestyle essays and 30 art images by my Norwegian Artist, Steve Henderson. Available at Amazon.com)

This Woman Writes (Online blog at www.ThisWomanWrites.areavoices.com and www.ThisWomanWrites.com)

Steve Henderson Fine Art (Online gallery of paintings by my Norwegian Artist, Steve Henderson at www.SteveHendersonFineArt.com) Steve sells his work as originals, signed limited edition prints, and open edition fine art prints. He also publishes a free weekly e-mail newsletter, Start Your Week with Steve, that focuses on happy, upbeat, and hopeful. You can sign up for this through the Newsletter button on the website.

You can find both me and Steve on our Facebook pages:

This   Woman   Writes   --
https://www.facebook.com/ThisWomanWrites

Steve   Henderson   Fine   Art   --
https://www.facebook.com/SteveHendersonFineArt

www.ingramcontent.com/pod-product-compliance
Lightning Source LLC
Chambersburg PA
CBHW051454170526
45166CB00001B/236